experimental
architecture
houses

First published in the United States of America in 2004
by UNIVERSE PUBLISHING
A Division of Rizzoli International Publications, Inc.
300 Park Avenue South
New York, NY 10010
www.rizzoliusa.com

Originally published by Links International, Barcelona, Spain
Copyright 2003 by
© Links International
Cover photograph © Nicholas Kane

Work Concept: Jacobo Krauel
Publisher: Carles Broto
Editorial Coordinator: Joan Fontbernat
Architectural Advisor: Pilar Chueca
Graphic Design and Production: Héctor Navarro
Layout Design: Dani González
Text: contributed by the architects and edited
by Jacobo Krauel and Amber Ockrassa

Printed in Spain. 2004

2004 2005 2006 2007/ 10 9 8 7 6 5 4 3 2 1

ISBN: 0-7893-1059-7

Library of Congress Catalog Control Number: 2003114940

experimental
architecture
houses

UNIVERSE

introduction

"There's no place like home," goes the adage, to which we might add "especially if yours is one of the houses shown on the following pages." Indeed, there is nothing standardized about these highly unconventional dwellings, which have been designed strictly for (and by) the adventurer at heart.

They are "experimental" in the sense that there were no existing prototypes to work from and that, in many cases, the designs break all the commonly-accepted rules of house architecture. In some cases, it was nothing more than a concept that formed the basis of the program (such is the case with the home patterned after the Möbius strip or the scheme based on Salvador Dalí's statements on the future of architecture); in others, the lifestyles of the clients themselves were the source of inspiration behind a personalized scheme - one house designed specifically for musicians takes on the shape of the inner ear!

The only trait the following projects have in common is that each radically defies convention in its own unique way.

To provide further depth and cohesion, we have also included an array of explanatory information and floor plans provided by the architects themselves.

Bjarne Marterbroek & MVRDV
Double House Utrecht
Utrecht, The Netherlands

In this Utrecht double villa the wall occupies a dominant position as a zigzagging partition between the two dwellings (and has been left in view on the exterior as a result). Paradoxically, it is virtually disregarded as a structural element.

The architects opted for a cube shape, vertically divided into two dwellings occupying a third and two thirds of the space respectively.

To give the occupants of the smaller block a sizeable living room, the living rooms of each dwelling intrude into the volume of the other. This gave rise to a meandering party wall that gave flexibility for the spatial organization of the villa.

The architects hark back here to building practices of times when the walls had to be structurally thick enough to allow hollows to be scooped out of them.

This villa is in effect a stacking of hollow cavities interconnected by open staircases and voids, the only enclosed areas being the bedrooms, small contained boxes suspended in space.

Almost none of the walls are positioned one above the other. Only the head elevations rise to the full height of the building. Columns were ruled out by the architects since they felt these would mar the spatial impact of the cavities. And as they wished to make the facade as transparent as possible with full-height windows, creative methods had to be devised to give the building sufficient stiffness. This play of forces was intimately resolved using pre-stressed beams, steel rods and cleverly positioned concrete balconies.

The levels in the right-hand dwelling create very fine loft-like open spaces organized in a horizontal sandwich. The left-hand dwelling is more labyrinthine. Its cavities are vertically arranged around an axis of two stacked but slightly staggered voids. From the kitchen on the ground floor the inhabitants can see right up to the roof eleven meters above.

If spatially interesting as living space, the long narrow rooms are not very practicable. For this reason, the living room on the third floor provides a welcome break from the verticality of this dwelling.

The bathroom with its fully glazed wall opens onto the roof terrace, a high parapet around the roof guaranteeing privacy though a section of it can be lowered for an unobstructed view of the park. And the roof terrace offers a permanent view of the cathedral spire.

A distinctive feature of the double villa is the façade. It is unusual in that it was not designed. The only finishing details in the façade are the sturdy wooden shuttering boards that clad the concrete sections.

Photographs: Daniel Mayer

The complete transparency of the façades is achieved by means of floor-to-ceiling openings. The metal frames of doors and windows acquire structural functions and work as loading-bearing elements.

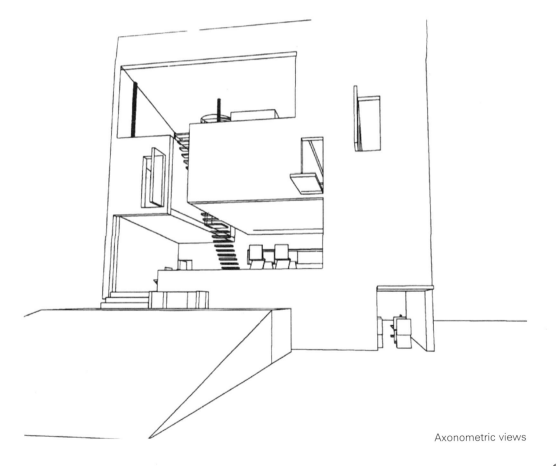

Axonometric views

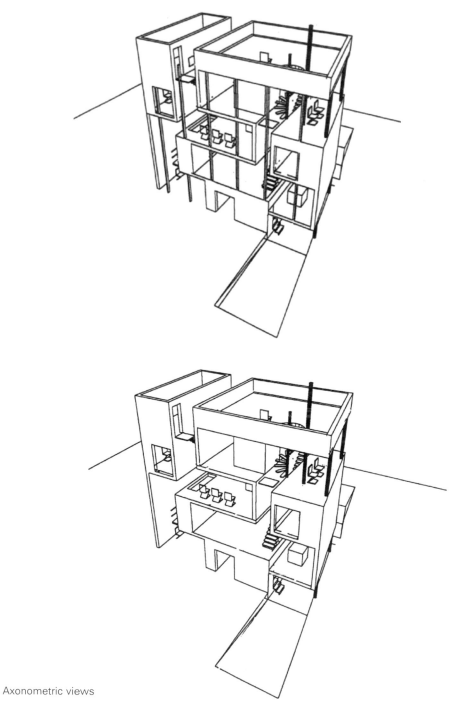

Axonometric views

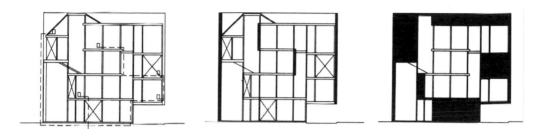

Functional schemes that show, from left to right, the drainage system, the structural stability in north-south direction and windowless façade planes.

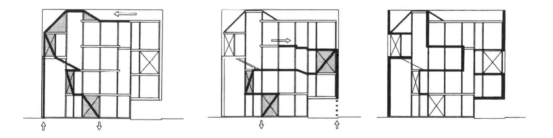

Sequence of schemes that show the general distribution of forces in the building and in the level 4 (left and center drawings) and party wall and head elevations.

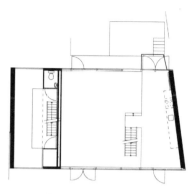

First floor plan

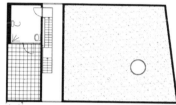

Upper level floor plan

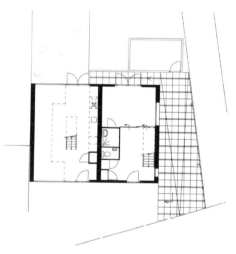

Ground floor plan

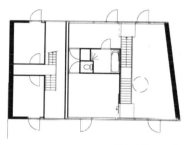

Third floor plan

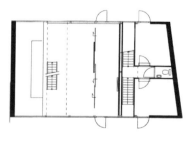

Second floor plan

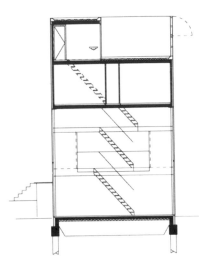
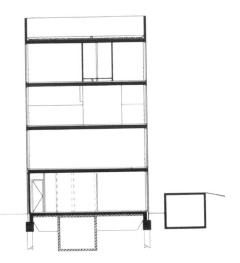

Cross sections

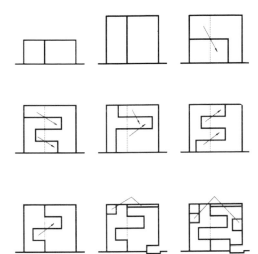

The different floors are intercommunicated by open staircases and are structured transparently, guaranteeing a flexible spatial organization.
The only closed rooms are the bedrooms, which seem to be small and surprising containers suspended in the space.

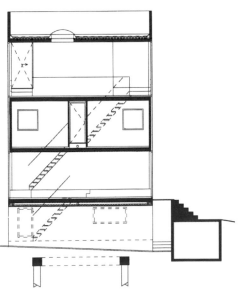

0 0.5 1 2

Cross section

Axonometric views

The dwelling pictured to the left is the more labyrinthine. Here, the living room is hollowed out of the neighbor's volume on the third floor thus providing a welcome break from the verticality of the dwelling.

The interiors of both dwellings are open and diaphanous. Columns, pillars and any kind of visual obstacle were ruled out by the architects. Also, the spaces are planned as very illuminated rooms, with full height windows.

Cross section

Ushida Findlay Partnership
Soft and Hairy House
Tsukuba, Japan

We were contacted by a young couple who were both architectural journalists. Intrigued by the provocative statements of Salvador Dalí on the architecture of the future, they requested a house which was soft and hairy.

More than a flight of fantasy, it was their attempt to link and affiliate spaces of different forms and contexts. It was an appropriation of surrealism, which released them from the socially cohesive, normative view of housing development in Japan.

In typology a hairy surface is one in which the continuous properties of surfaces are studied through flows. The request for "soft and hairiness" was read as a mixture. Theirs was not a purely esoteric desire; rather it was radical, polemic and political.

The form of the house embodies the couple, his head and her head face each other across the entryway and their child lies between. The internal plan is a landscape of the familiar and unfamiliar.

Of all the arts, architecture has been the most distant from surrealism because of its realistic economic basis. Even rare examples of surrealist architecture, such as the Beistegui apartment by Corbusier and Casa Maraparte by Libera, seem to be client instigated.

Surrealism was an attempt to overcome "reality" framed by the illusions of nationality, currency, culture and community. This was achieved by liberating and sharing individual illusions by referring to psychoanalysis and Marxism and considering dreams, insanity and automatism.

In the status quo where "reality" goes beyond our imagination and obscures the boundary between real and virtual, we often see images derived from surrealist art entering our daily lives. In other words, "real" life imitates art. In order to solve the problems of the house building type –in this kind of status quo– it is effective to make a space/container of life floating in between the "virtual" (private illusion / subconsciousness) and "real" economical and social substance of architecture. Conventional methods of architecture have never addressed these problems.

Dali's enormous body of work is recognized as the materialization of dream. If Japanese minimalist design, the currently dominant architectural force, purports to "de-materialize the real" this attempt may be called a "materialization of dream" in the manner of Dalí. The architects have tried to envisage a "reality" which can exist by scattering decoded architectural and non-architectural elements in one space. Inside, a concrete tube spiralling around a courtyard, a blue egg-shaped bathroom and amorphous blue stones bearing the inscriptions, "dream" "dread" and "desire" float in the space. A strange tactility pervades the interior; its walls are swathed in canvas, a door is wrapped in fake fur, and hairy foliage overhangs. But this new "reality" has a vague periphery as it has shed the "real" of the outside world.

Photographs: Katsuhisa Kida

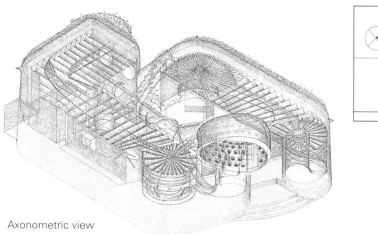

Axonometric view

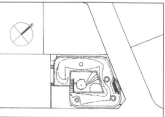

Site plan

The foliage occupying the entire roof of this dwelling spills out over delicately curved walls.
Inside, the building displays the complexity and beauty of organic forms in all of the spaces, which are arranged so as to receive the light from the central patio.

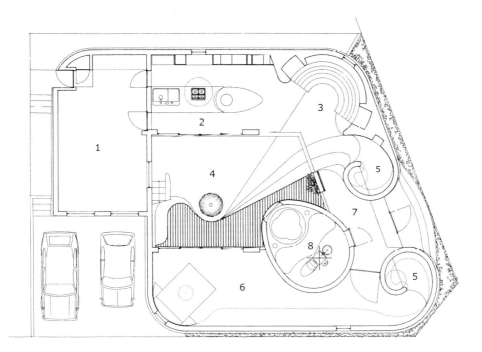

Floor plans

1. Play room
2. Dining-kitchen
3. Living
4. Courtyard
5. Study
6. Bedroom
7. Entrance
8. Bathroom

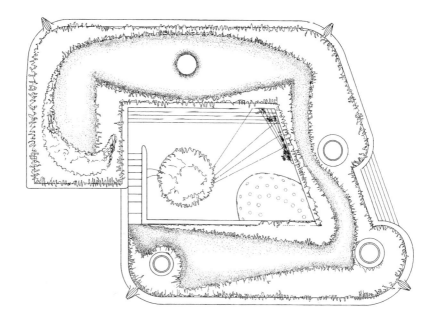

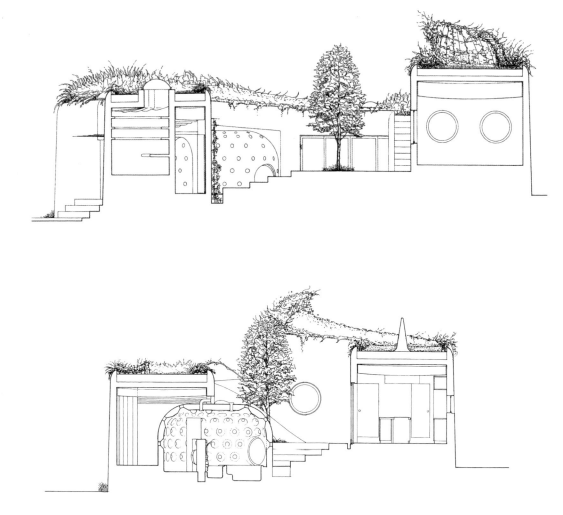

Elevations

The bathroom has been designed in a curious spherical shape. Its placement, in a corner of the dwelling's inner patio, allows it to directly receive the natural light filtering through the small openings covering the surface.

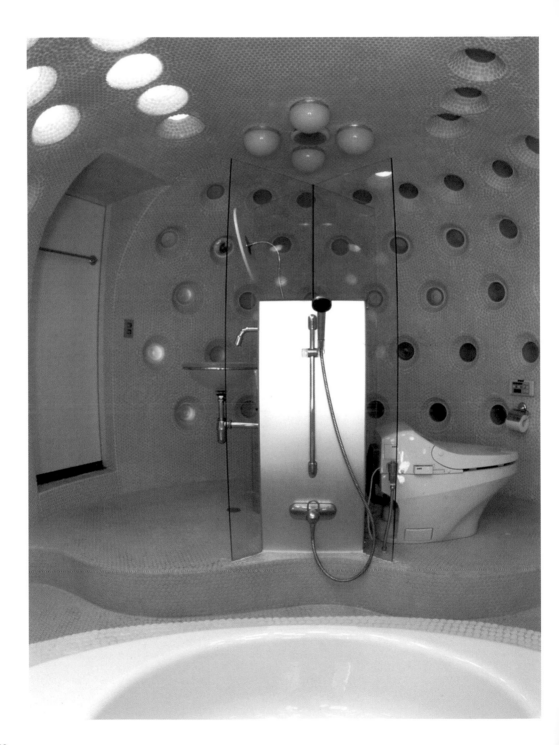

Engelen Moore
House in Redfern
Sydney, Australia

This two-story house has been built on a vacant block of land formerly occupied by two terrace houses, in a street of houses, warehouses and apartments of varying ages and scales. The local council insisted that it read as two terrace type houses rather than as a warehouse. The front elevation is divided into two vertical bays. The major horizontal elements align with, and each bay relates proportionally to, the adjoining terrace houses. The internal planning reflects this two-bay arrangement at the front, while the rear elevation expresses the full 19 ³/₄ ft high by 23 ft wide internal volume. There was a very limited budget for this project, so a simple strategy was developed to construct a low-cost shell comprised of a steel portal framed structure with concrete block external skins to the long sides, lined with plasterboard internally. The front and rear parapets and blade walls are clad with compressed fiber cement sheet. This shell is painted white throughout. Within this white shell are placed a series of more refined and rigorously detailed elements differentiated by their aluminum or gray paint finish.

The front elevation is composed of six vertical panels: the lower level is clad in Alucobond aluminum composite sheet; the panel to the left comprises the 10 ³/₄ ft high front door; and the 3 panels on the right side together form the garage door. The upper level is made up of operable extruded aluminum louvers, enabling it to be adjusted from completely transparent to opaque.

The 19 ³/₄ ft high west-facing glass wall is made up of the six individual panels, which slide and stack to one side allowing the entire rear elevation to be opened up. This not only spatially extends the interior into the courtyard, but, in combination with the louvered front elevation, allows exceptional control of cross ventilation to cool the house in the summer time, while allowing very good solar penetration to warm the house in winter. In summer this western glass wall is screened from the sun by a large eucalyptus tree on the adjoining property.

Photographs: Ross Honeysett

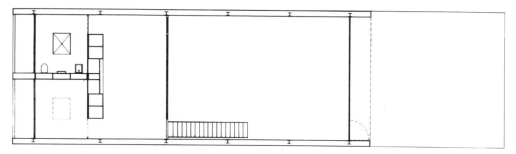

First floor plan

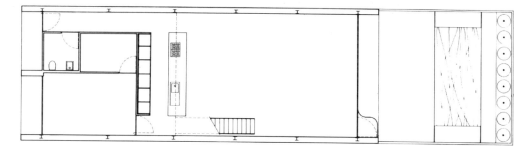

Ground floor plan

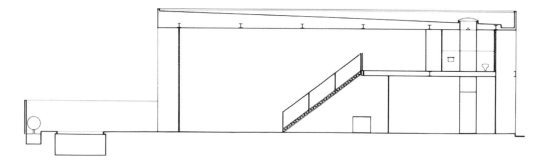

Longitudinal section

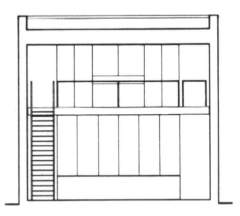

Cross section

When the six glass panels forming the rear
façade are wide open, they extend the interior of
the dwelling towards the garden.

The furniture was designed by the architects. The basic premises were that it should be cost efficient and light-weight for easy mobility. The rooms of the upper floor are fitted with mobile aluminum shutters that can be completely transparent or opaque.

Santiago Calatrava
Buchen Housing Estate
Würenlingen, Switzerland

This residential colony is located very close to Zürich, on the edge of the small town of Würenlingen. Coexisting with other developments in an open landscape, this small series of homes is positioned parallel to the main road.

The project called for the construction of 24 free-standing dwellings, to be arranged in two twelve-unit rows flanking a square, and three groups of six attached houses to the south of the site, right at the edge of a wooded area. The client, Remer Real Estate, specified that concrete be the main material used in the entire colony, for which reason all the external façades are constructed with prefabricated concrete elements. The shape of the building –with the top story having a wider floor area than the lower two– is a result of the restrictive conditions of the site. In this way the amount of land occupied by each unit is reduced to a minimum, allowing views through the complex in the case of the isolated houses, while the interplay of light and shade is enhaced.

The land drops down slightly from the woods, and the slope is used to ground the section and create a series of exterior spaces at different levels. On the low northern side the ground floor opens onto the spatious main entrance portico, while on the other side, staircases –one for each succesive pair of units– connect the back doors to the wood's raised land. The backyards on this level are accessed directly from the living rooms, which stretch from front to rear.

The rooms of a more public or communal nature –the dining rooms and entries at ground level and the living rooms on the upper floor– all face the double-height portico, creating a façade that is more glazed than not, the only element separating one unit from another being a narrow concrete panel. The volumes containing the top floor bedrooms –a total of three per unit– look like ocular cavities, eyes staring vacantly at the landscape. A stylized pillar situated at the transversal axis of each dwelling sustains the load of this top floor obliquely, and gives the complex its defining image.

Photographs: Hans Ege

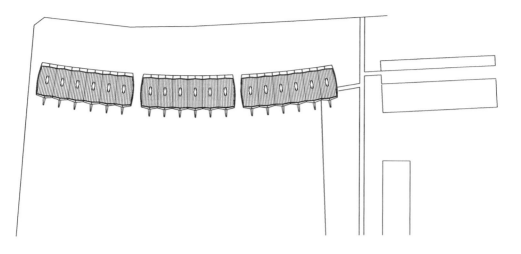

Site plan

The complex, built mainly in concrete, runs parallel to the main road. The outer walls are made of prefabricated concrete elements.

Perspective

Exploded view

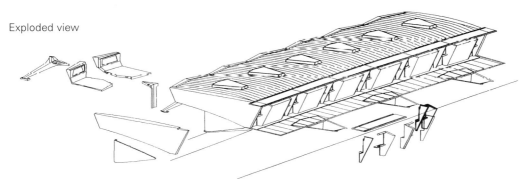

Section B-B

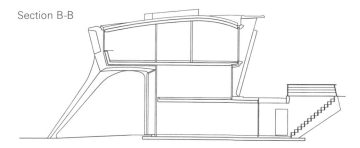

The dwellings were fitted into the sloping terrain creating exterior spaces on several levels. The upper volume housing the bedrooms is supported by stylized pillars that transfer the load obliquely to the ground and define the external appearance of the complex.

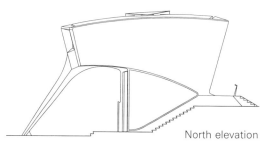

North elevation

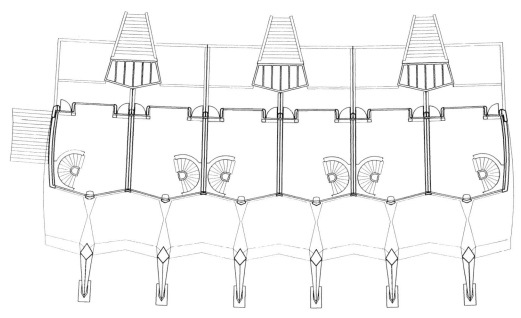

First floor plan

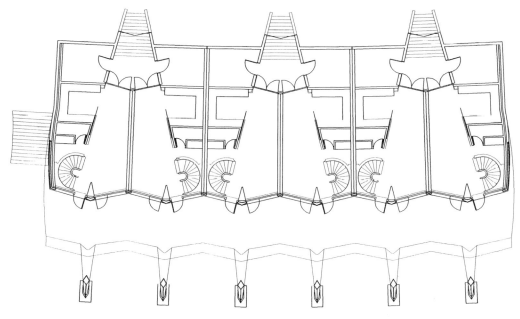

Ground floor plan

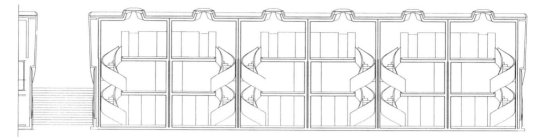

Longitudinal section

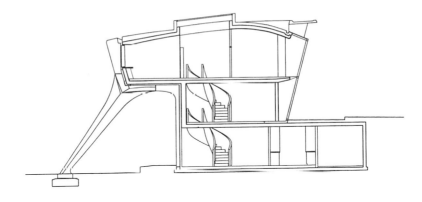

The more public premises open onto the double-height portico that is common to all the dwellings. Above this space the upper volumes of the dwellings protrude, separated only by thin screens.

Rem Koolhaas
Dutch House
The Netherlands

Marking the termination and final frontier of the ice age, a moraine remains as a Dutch hill, fifty meters above sea level.

The 53,820 ft^2 site is located here, in a forest of pine on fine golden beach sand. Aside from the unstable ground conditions, specific site requirements included a height restriction of four meters above the adjacent road and an excessive limitation of buildable area. Literal interpretations of these givens dictated the maximum frame; manipulations of the terrain were subsequent. A driveway was carved out to ensure efficiency of access.

The program consists of facilities for two permanent residents and their three grown-up daughters, who visit occasionally. To fade the presence of their absence, a programmatic split was introduced, materialized by the slab held by one house, while holding the other. The focus of the architects was how to translate two different conditions of occupation related to specific site conditions as autonomous elements with moments of interaction, and how to compress a maximum program into a minimum of formal gestures.

At ground level, one wrapping wall defines a continuity of interior spaces and patios for the daughters' quarters, which are introverted and grounded spaces.

The floating deck supports a crystallized container of the parents' program. A single hinge —the pivoting bridge/horizontal door— feeds both bed-room units with patio above, service entry below.

The wall itself contains all functional elements, dictating adjacent activity but leaving the surrounding space free within the glass box, which is physically detached from but visually inclusive of the surrounding landscape. Various treatments of glass and shadings manipulate this relationship according to the program and orientation.

The node of the house is a central ramp providing visual and functional connection between the two counterparts.

Photographs: Christian Ritchers

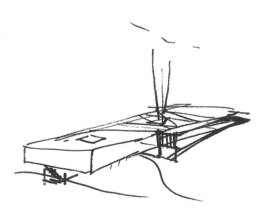

A surface that floats above the land serves as a base for the glazed volume that contains the parents' rooms.

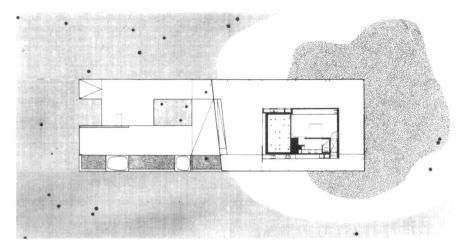

Upper level plan

The external appearance of the dwelling is dominated by the volumetrics and by the different types of glazing and other solar protection.

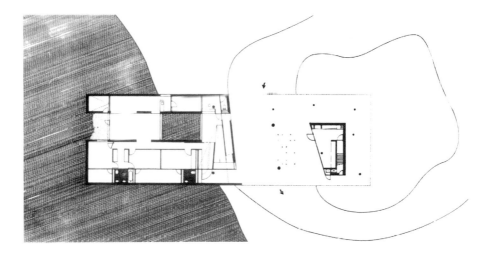

Lower level plan

Cross sections through the access ramp

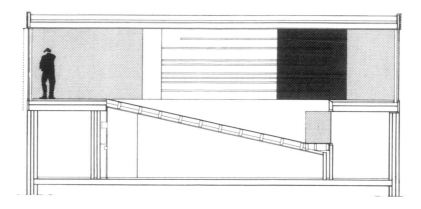

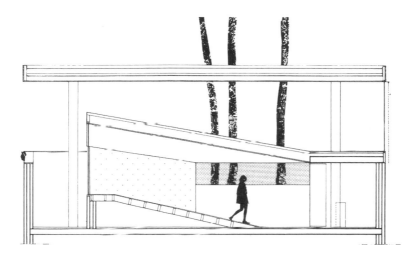

The ramp that provides access to the dwelling connects the two parts into which it is divided both physically and visually.

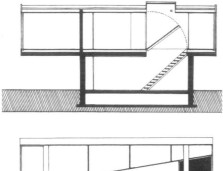

Cross sections

0 1 2 4

Longitudinal sections

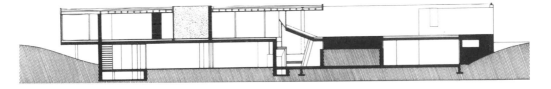

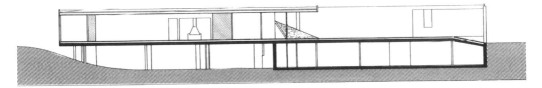

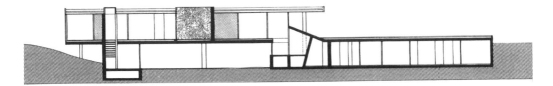

Ushida Findlay Partnership
Polyphony
Osaka, Japan

Located on a site in a suburb of Osaka created for the Exhibition of 1970, this original dwelling was conceived for a couple of musicians and their children. Music and architecture seem to converge in this building, which bears a certain resemblance to the structure of the inner ear. Polyphony is a musical term that refers to the overlapping of sounds in a composition. Authors like Bartok, who incorporated popular songs into his work, and John Cage, who introduced the sound created by the public and the space, paved the way for contemporary music, which uses sampling and mixes to create sound atmospheres full of superimposed nuances. The combination of sound and construction has a long tradition in Japan, where materials and vegetation (such as bamboo to transform the wind into music and attract birds) are often chosen for the acoustic effect that they give. In the design of this dwelling, conceived so that its inhabitants could experience the sounds of the environment as part of a total sensorial experience, the aim was to create a space that had a correlation with the repetitive acoustic cycles.

The ground plan of the dwelling is based on a geometric pattern on which circles of 11 $\frac{1}{4}$ ft in diameter are traced around a main circle, achieving an original form similar to that of a slightly curved sausage. This winding tube is cut diagonally, so that the solid is gradually transformed into a void. The overlapping of cylinders to generate a space of multiple layers is directly related to the effect of the chords formed by superimposed sounds. In accordance with the visual experience of the space, the aim was to create a sound landscape in which a range of unexpected acoustic effects could be heard. This was achieved by means of curved walls forming a series of corridors that seem to whisper and give off strange echoes similar to those achieved when holding a shell to one's ear. These curved forms are repeated in the whole house and make the interior an enveloping place full of winding corners in which the furniture and the openings play a major role.

Photographs: Katsuhisa Kida, Takeshi Taira

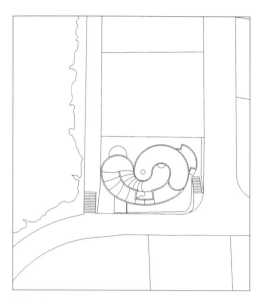

Site plan

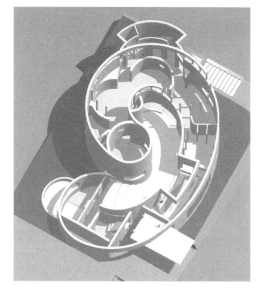

Axonometric view

The ground plan of the dwelling is based on a geometric pattern on which circles of 11 $\frac{1}{4}$ ft diameter are traced around a main circle. This creates a winding, tubular space that appears to be cut diagonally so that the solid is gradually transformed into a void.

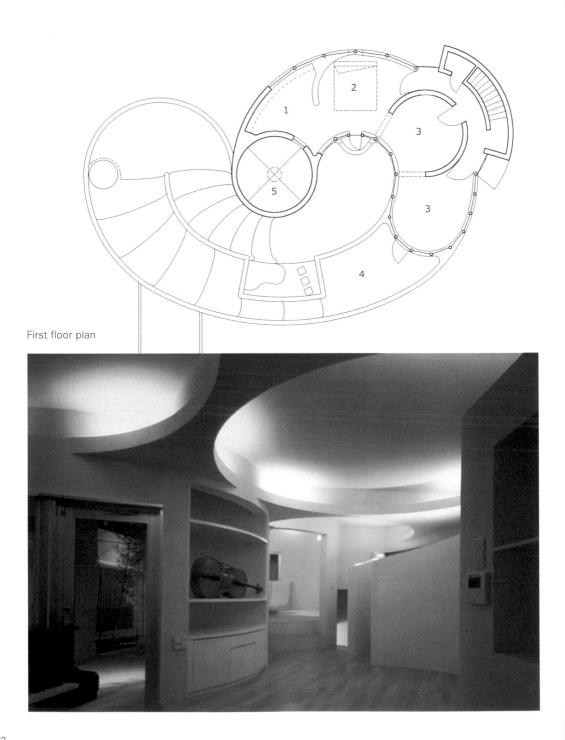

First floor plan

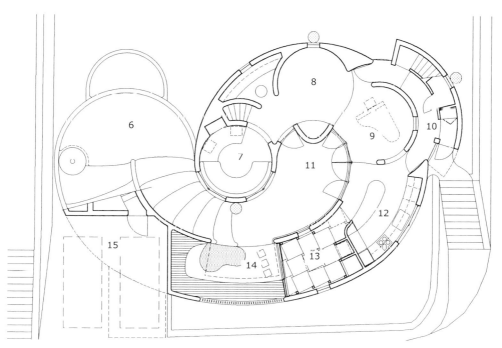

Ground floor plan

1. Wardrobe	6. Kids' patio	11. Courtyard
2. Main bedroom	7. Audio zone	12. Kitchen-dining
3. Bedroom	8. Family zone	13. Japanese room
4. Terrace	9. Piano zone	14. Garden
5. Void	10. Entrance	15. Garage

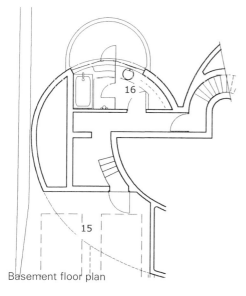

Basement floor plan

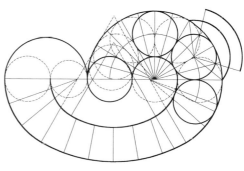

Geometric diagram

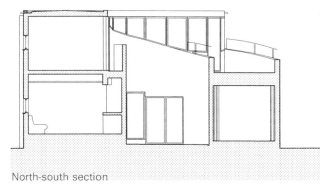

The curved walls were intended to create a landscape in which the inhabitants could experience the sounds of the environment as part of a total sensorial experience.

North-south section

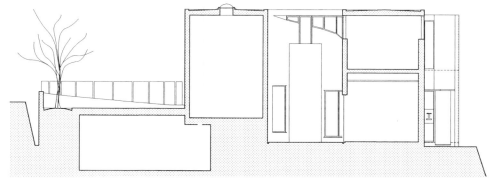

East-west section

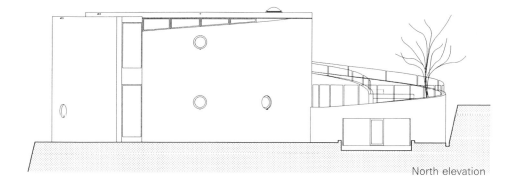

North elevation

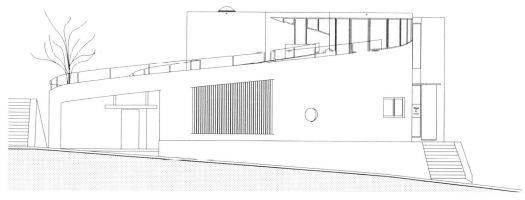

South elevation

Graham Phillips
Skywood House
Middlesex, UK

This home's plot, etched into a densely populated area, was subject to zoning laws which restricted the surface area available for construction to 2,691 ft². The architect set out to create a "glass box" in the forest, a structure whose boundaries between interior and exterior would be blurred, where water would play a leading role.

The house, lying before the shores of a lake, is reached via a black gravel walkway which winds around the house, ending at the main patio at the back. The building rests on a gray limestone plinth, its bare, unadorned surface highlighting its simple shapes. Frameless glass doors covered by a pergola, a design echoed in the entrance to the garage, form the main entryway. A noteworthy element in the exterior space is the main chimney, which hides the drainage system, pipes and ventilation system within a single unit. The dwelling is unified by long walls which reach beyond the enclosed spaces toward the lake and surrounding terrain, thereby defining footpaths. This minimalist expression contrasts with the wealth of the landscape, creating a serene, yet wondrous, experience.

The dwelling is enclosed by two glass wings, the first of which, at a height of 9³/₄ ft, forms the volume containing the four bedrooms and their respective bathrooms. This module comprises one of the sides of a completely enclosed garden, which has a square lawn lying over a border of black gravel.

The glass volume which houses the sitting room is the tallest, thereby highlighting the steel sheet of which the floating roof is comprised. The main space enjoys breathtaking views across the lake to the west, toward the island, as much a focal point by night as by day.

The tiling of the sitting room continues outward toward the garden, through a glass façade, blurring the boundaries between interior and exterior. This space is organized like a double square: the sitting room is defined by a 38.75 ft² carpet centered over limestone flooring. Its motif of a square framed within another background is seen again in the inside patio and the garden at the back. In the kitchen/dining room, a combination of sliding panels and two moveable tables allow a distribution which can be altered according to its user's needs. The kitchen and dining room may be combined or they can be separated to create different settings.

Photographs: Nigel Young

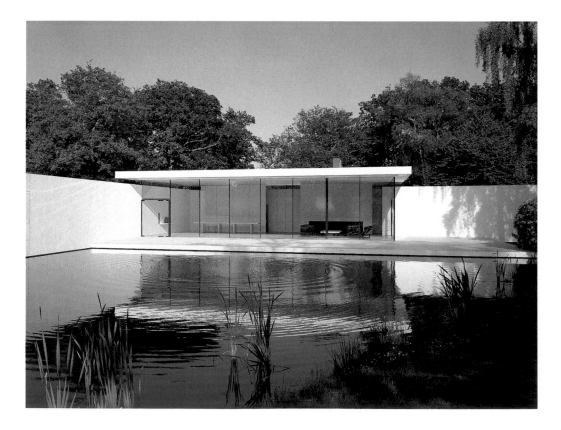

The artificial lake, a huge pond with geotextile protection layers under a foot of soil, is supplied by an 80-foot deep well and is sharply framed by the lawn. Reflections from the water create a constantly changing array of light inside the dwelling.

1. Entry
2. Drive
3. Lake
4. Bridge
5. Waterwall
6. Courtyard
7. Walled Garden
8. Terrace
9. Logstore

Site plan

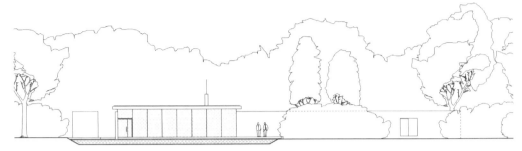

West elevation

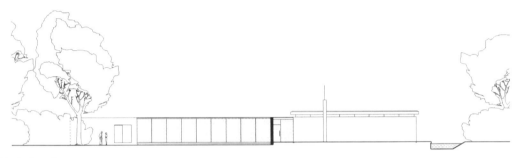

East elevation

Limestone and glass, used both inside and out, confer homogeneity on the building and continuity between the exterior and interior.

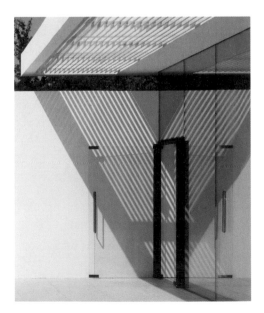

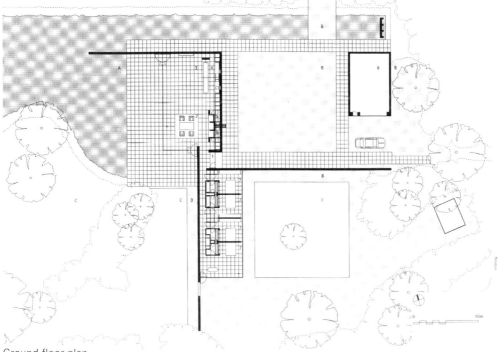

Ground floor plan

The windows, conceived as openings in the walls, have disappeared and been replaced by skylights with a mechanical ventilating system.

The entrance hall enjoys privileged views of the garden and artificial lake, which fits perfectly into the terrain and comprises an extension of the dwelling.

East-west section through lake, living room and courtyard

East-west section through master bedroom and garden

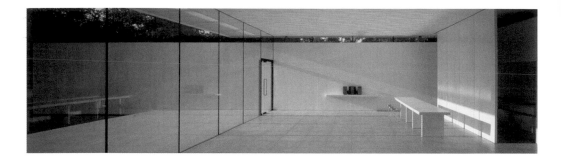

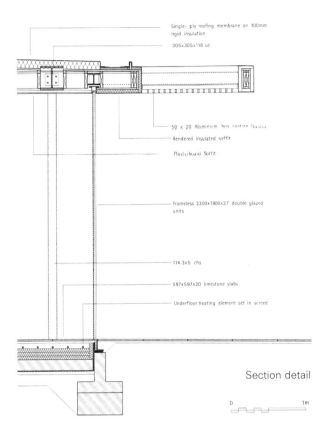

Single- ply roofing membrane on 100mm
rigid insulation

305x305x118 uc

50 x 20 Aluminium box coping louvres

Rendered insulated soffit

Plasterboard Soffit

Frameless 3300x1800x37 double glazed
units

114.3x5 chs

597x597x20 limestone slabs

Underfloor heating element set in screed

Section detail

0   1m

The entirety of the water, electrical
and ventilation systems are operated
through a single vertical duct, while
the heating system is underground,
thereby avoiding the need for radia-
tors. The furniture and other decorative elements have been custom-
designed for this home.

Linda Searl, Joseph Valerio
Ohio House
Chicago, Illinois, USA

The streets are the essence of the city. They are a community symbol, a place of encounter. In them lies the tension, even the violence. Urban streets encapsulate everything that we cannot find in the suburbs: light, energy and activity. In a city like Chicago, with such a clear grid plan, the crossroads are critical. It could be said that everything happens at the corners.

Instead of being articulated axially toward each of the streets that converge at a point, the Ohio Street House takes as its axis the same point (the corner), thus capturing the energy that is concentrated at the intersection of the grid.

The design of this dwelling is based on two superimposed forms: a circle and a square that share the same centroid. The dwelling is at the same time open and shielded. On one hand, the construction reflects the discipline of the street; on the other, it receives and absorbs all the unexpected events that happen in it.

Highly expressive materials were used in the construction of the house, underlining the division between the ground floor and the upper floors. The lower level has a brickwork cladding which does not contrast with the surrounding dwellings. On the upper floors, however, the exterior was clad in grooved metal plates. The street-side façade seems to be a continuation of that of the ground floor, but the rear part of the dwelling is solved in a different way: with a semicircle.

In the house, the more public elements of the floor plan are developed in parallel to the two streets that form the corner. The living room is aligned with Oakley Street and curves to form the space devoted to the kitchen and dining room, parallel to Ohio Street. Inside this "L" is the staircase. The public spaces are located in the corner facing the street, while the private environments are located in the opposite corner. The central staircase leads to the upper levels. The first floor houses the main bedroom, a dressing room and the main bathroom. The second floor houses a bedroom, a bathroom and a large work area.

Photographs: Barbara Karant; Karant+Associates

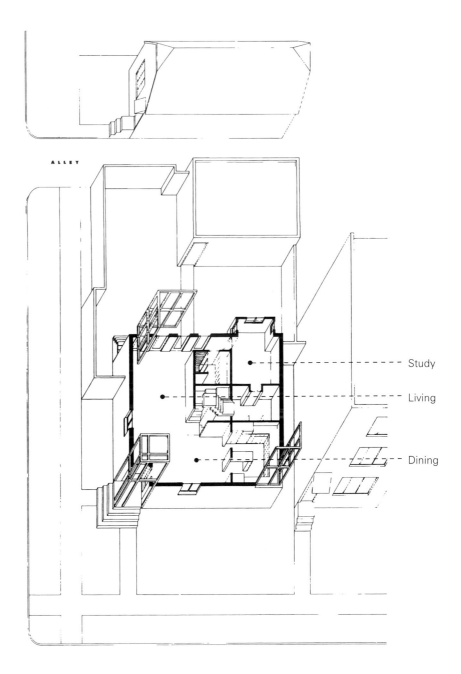

ALLEY

Study

Living

Dining

The lower level has a square floor plan, while those of the upper levels are semicircular. This difference is also reflected in the materials used for the external lining of each level: white paint on the brick at street level and grooved metal plate on the first and second floors.

The dwelling was conceived as a polyvalent space, with closely related, almost overlapping atmospheres in an interplay of volumes and heights. Through this spatial and volumetric heterogeneity, the architect is able to diffuse the dividing barriers in the distribution of the interior.

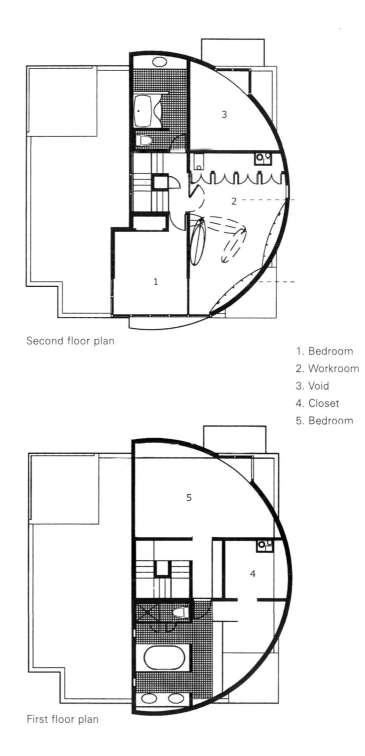

Second floor plan

1. Bedroom
2. Workroom
3. Void
4. Closet
5. Bedroom

First floor plan

The interplay of volumes on the exterior is reflected inside the dwelling. Wooden panels separate the area of the dining room and the kitchen.

Shinichi Ogawa & Associates
Glass House
Hiroshima, Japan

The building is located in the area of Hiroshima known as Nishi Ward, which lies in the western part of the city. This area sits on the estuary of the Hachiman River where it flows into the Seto Inland Sea.

This is a very pure and geometrical volume, a minimal and open glass box that contains at the same time the house and studio of the architect Shinichi Ogawa.

The project is based on $9^{3}/_{4}$ feet, three-dimensional grid and takes the simple form of a box measuring $19^{3}/_{4}$ x $49^{1}/_{4}$ x $39^{1}/_{2}$ ft. The volume is divided into four parts along its Z-axis, with the two uppermost blocks ($19^{3}/_{4}$ x $49^{1}/_{4}$ x $19^{3}/_{4}$ ft) forming the third floor, where the architectural office is located, and the two lower blocks constituting the first and second floor living spaces.

Furniture and partitions divide the living areas and the spaces have a neutral quality, allowing flexibility with respect to changing functional requirements.

The building is wrapped in transparent glass on all four façades, thus strongly contributing to making the interior a very sunny and fresh space during the daytime. Nevertheless, all the spaces can be enclosed, if desired, using movable insulating screens, which also alter the perception of the building from the outside.

Photographs: Hiroyuki Hirai/Shigeo Ogawa

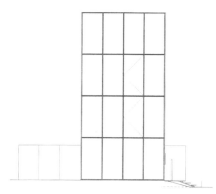

East elevation

North elevation

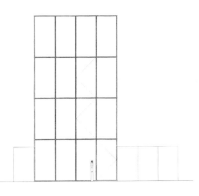

West elevation

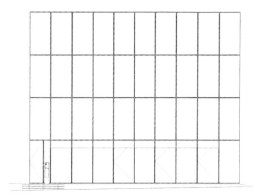

South elevation

The house takes on the form of a glass box measuring $19^{3/4}$ x $49^{1/4}$ x $39^{1/2}$ ft. Vertically, it is divided into four parts. The office occupies the two uppermost volumes while the two lower areas hold the living areas.

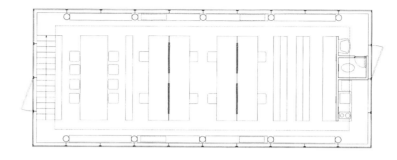

Third floor plan

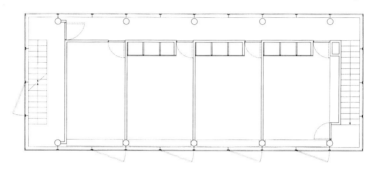

Second floor plan

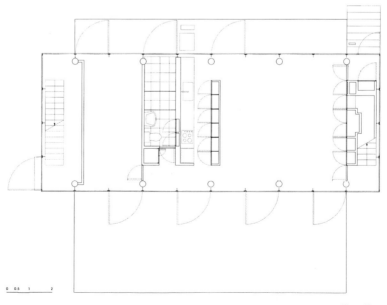

0 0.5 1   2

First floor plan

The building is wrapped in transparent glass on all four façades, thus strongly contributing to making the interior a very clear and sunny space during the daytime.

Movable insulating screens increase the level of privacy and solar protection on the four transparent glass façades.

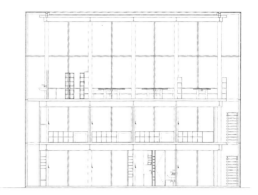

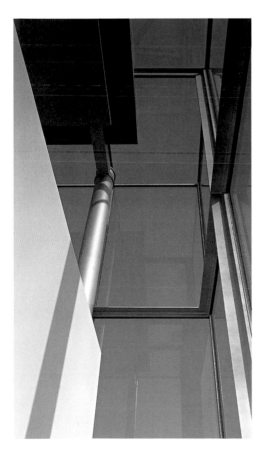

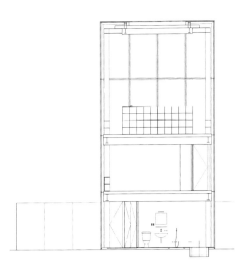

Cross section

The open character of the building allows splendid views of the Hachiman River from even the remotest corner of the interior.

Klaus Sill & Jochen Keim
Apartment and Office Building
Rathenow, Germany

The building converted by Klaus Sill and Jochen Keim was built over a century ago, although it was later modified by joining the front area to the courtyard. Now, the building has been homogeneously integrated into an environment that is distinguished by the walls of the block and a well thought-out concept that makes it suitable for working and living.

The courtyard building had fallen into a state of ruin in the last few decades: some walls had collapsed and others were in danger of collapsing.

The decision was made to conserve only one old dwelling and a warehouse, two elements which were located at the north-west end of the plot that were considered to be worth retaining. As part of the project, a major installation was built inside the block to serve as a landscaped area and playground for the tenants of the front building. Also, thanks to this arrangement, it was possible to cover the objectives stipulated in the city of Rathenow's zoning regulations concerning the separation between blocks and foundations.

The conjunction between offices and dwellings was achieved by means of a distribution in which the upper floors were reserved for the dwellings. Thus, the ground floor and first floor contain the cubes (12 modules) that house the offices of a firm of engineers with twenty employees. The second floor is composed of three maisonettes of about 646 and 970 ft^2.

Two united surfaces were used for the firm of engineers because the building protrudes about $14^{3}/_{4}$ ft into the courtyard. This extension is formed by two conference rooms, an audio-visual room, archive, kitchen and toilet.

Photographs: Christof Gebler & Klaus Sill

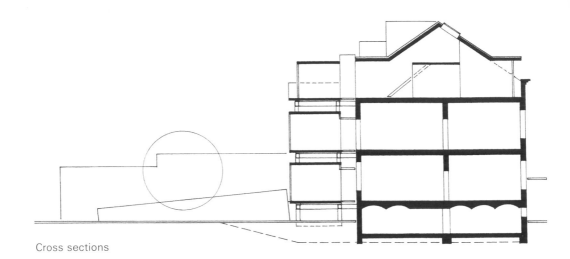

Cross sections

The project drew on the existing buildings and the surroundings for its defining characteristics. It brings together the functions of dwelling and workplace in a way that is more in line with the current lifestyle.

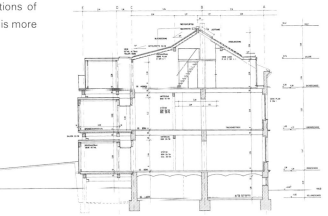

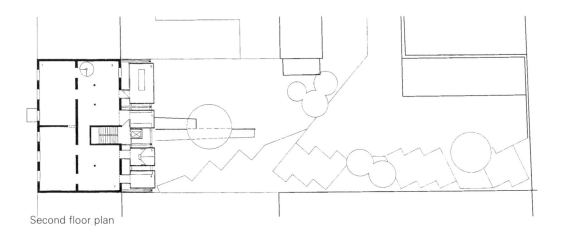

Second floor plan

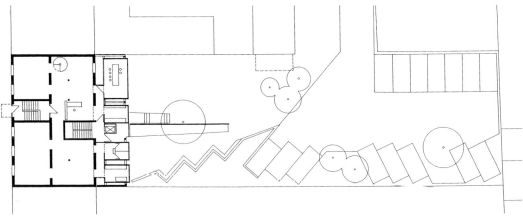

First floor plan

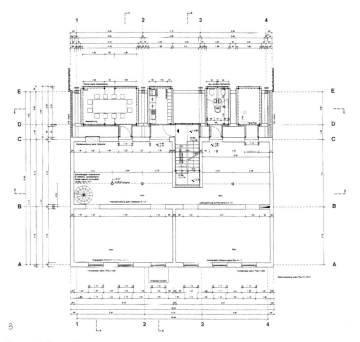

Second floor plan

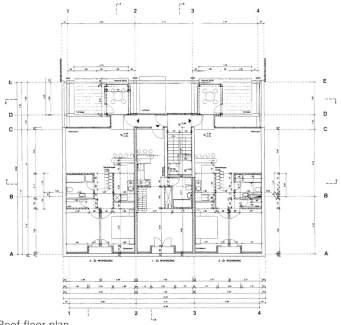

Roof floor plan

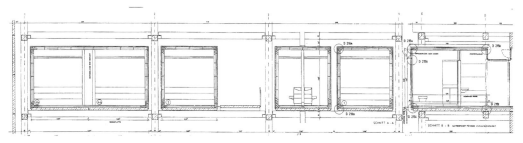

Sections A-A B-B

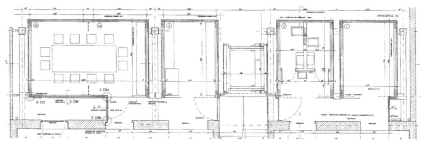

Ground floor plan

Construction of the roof and walls.
Axonometric view

1. 0.79" corrugated aluminum
3. 4.72" thermal insulation
4. Waterproof layer
5. 4.72" steel plate floor
6. Façade of stiles and rails
7. Insulated glass

Construction of the floor

8. Linoleum
10. 3" thermal insulation

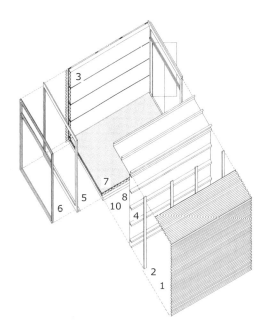

For economic and technical reasons, these modules were built 310 miles from the site as they were of a suitable size to be transported. They were set into a prefabricated reinforced concrete skeleton for fire protection.

Daniele Marques & Bruno Zurkirchen
Haus Kraan Lang
Emmenbrücke, Switzerland

The plot for which the single-family dwelling was to be designed is located in an area with a heterogeneous planning situation, a zone of agglomeration in which the urban fabric gives way to the countryside. There are buildings with different uses in the immediate vicinity: a farm building, cubic zigzag apartment blocks built in the sixties, and a concrete single-family dwelling.

The aim of the architectural design was to respond to the planning regulations by means of two floors consisting of an ephemeral container in opposition to the solid constructions.

Both the ground floor containing the living area and the upper floor containing the bedrooms are south facing. The living area faces a covered veranda that is slightly lower than the top of the sliding windows, thus making full use of natural light. The north side is closed in response to the railway line located in the immediate vicinity.

The position of the container, in exact relation to the neighboring concrete single-family dwelling, is intended to define an exterior space belonging to both houses. The single-family dwelling is prefabricated, the constructional system being based on large panels for light constructions and pillars resting on a pedestal in the basement. It is covered with untreated trapezoidal aluminum sheet. This aluminum cladding was used for all the exterior surfaces including the roof. The remaining wooden constructional elements were left untreated, except for a wax coating.

Photographs: Daniel Mayer

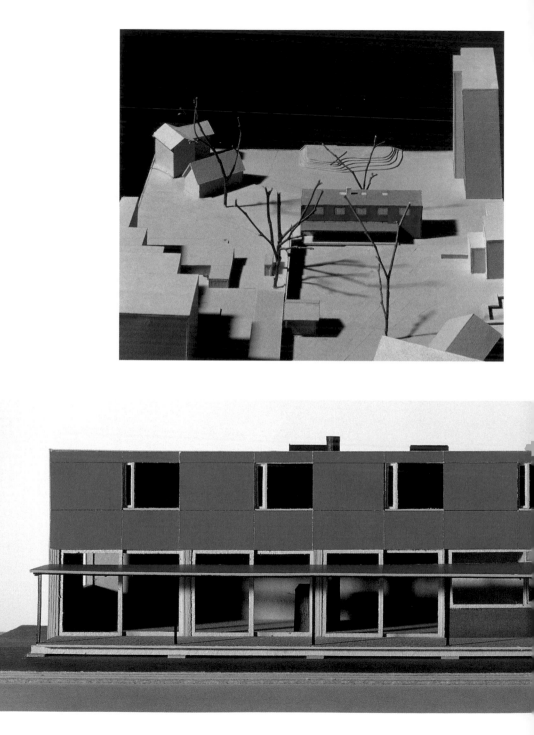

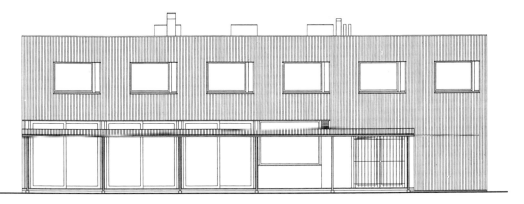

South façade

A study of the project's surroundings enabled the architectural team to define the spatial characteristics of the building. The aim was to distinguish the project from the progressive development of this formerly rural area, which is now a total planning chaos. The site plan shows how the articulation with the neighboring concrete house manages to create a more formalized exterior space.

Site plan

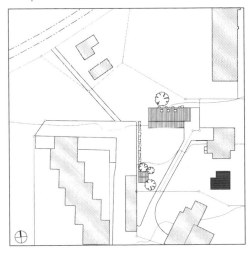

North side: the façade is practically blind, which responds to the nearby railway line, provides privacy from the large adjoining apartment block and increases the thermal comfort of the house.

East façade

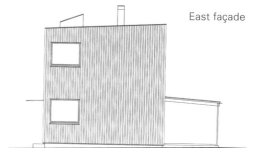

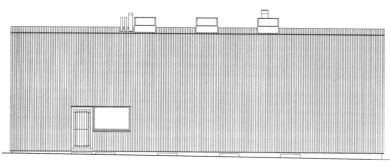

North façade

The large aluminum panels that recall industrial containers create an unexpected and subversive effect in the context and give nobility to the house despite their low cost and ephemeral appearance.

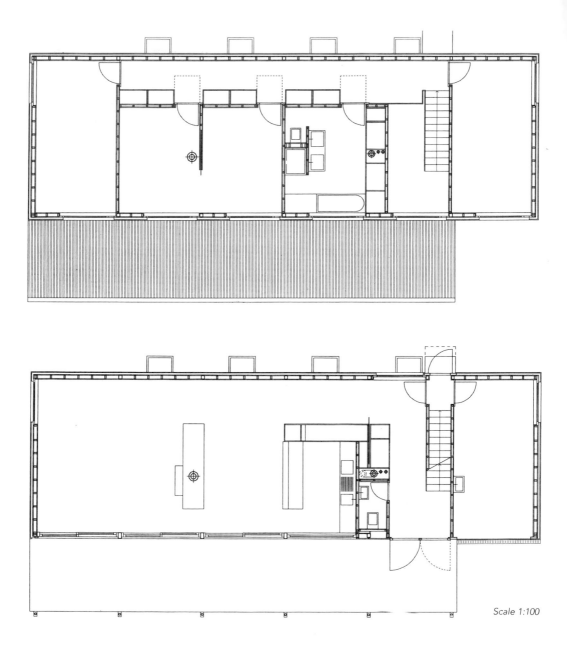

Scale 1:100

The large rectangle of the container is regulated with great simplicity and rationality by a grid in six equal divisions that correspond to the interior partition walls and the pillars of the portico on the south facade. The width of the portico preserves a certain privacy on the ground floor, screening it from the overlooking apartment blocks.

West section

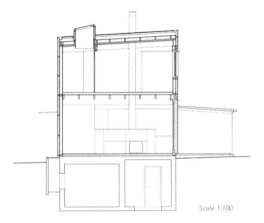

Scale 1:100

The interiors emanate a certain Loosian sensitivity: great importance is given to the materials, their natural use and their visual impact. The association between the metal, wood (untreated and waxed) and glass (with its reflections, brilliance and transparency) provide a tone of luxury and warmth in contrast to the external appearance.

Jones Studio, Inc
Walner Residence
Scottsdale, Arizona, USA

The shape of the home –a parallelogram built on two levels– results from key elements offered by the site. These include a boulder pile in the foreground, the western exposure, views of distant city lights, and the relationship of the site to the street. Behind the house the 85-foot long negative edge lap pool echoes the shape of the house.

Like a giant bird poised for flight, the home appears ready to soar above the Arizona desert. The home is clad in quartz colored titanium zinc roof and wall panels. The elongated roofline combined with the cantilevered steel structure of the main level effectively suspends the house above the desert. The drama of the super-extended roof edge began with the practical need to shade the high percentage glass walls.

At the upper level, the west windows incorporate mitered-glass corners, like a fish aquarium, providing uninterrupted views. Multiple areas for relaxing and dining allow for flexibility and accommodate the owner's extended family. Custom clear maple cabinetry accents the kitchen and houses the media center. The aluminum grating of the deck reflects the evening illumination and is comfortably cool even on hot days.

The architect-designed carpet complements the space and matches the circular cocktail table (also custom-designed by the architect) whose two legs pierce its glass top and culminate in candleholders. A suspended fireplace with its pleated-glass curtain can be viewed from inside the house or out.

On the lower level a glass wall pivots open to extend the inside to the outside, providing ventilation and access to the lower deck and pool area, which is shaded by the cantilevered balcony above. The 3,800 ft^2 structure is constructed primarily of insulated and sandblasted concrete block, structural steel, glass, and titanium zinc. Titanium zinc is lightweight, easy to install, requires zero maintenance, and will last a lifetime. Also, because the house was designed to "float" above the desert, the architects did not want to use any materials (such as masonry) that would increase the weight of the cantilevered structure. Therefore, they utilized a light-weight skin that could patina naturally and blend with the desert surroundings.

A pan formed standing seam system accentuates form and profiles the folded wall/roof planes without the interruption of ridge flashing. The standing seams are continuous from roof to wall with individual knuckle caps at each joint. The flexibility and highly durable characteristics of solid zinc provide virtually unlimited opportunities for the creative and expressive architect and value-conscious owner.

Photographs: Timothy Hursley

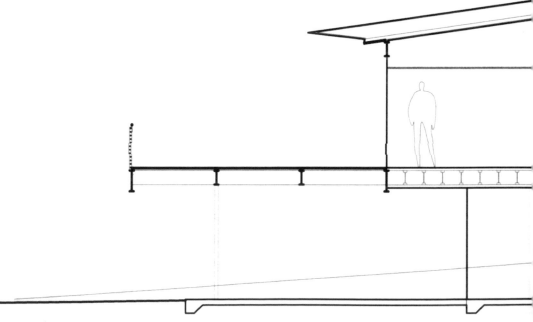

Cross section

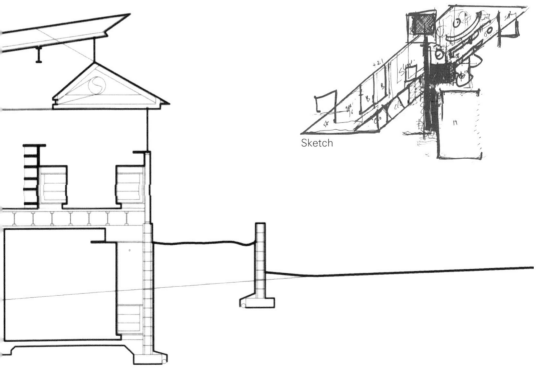

Sketch

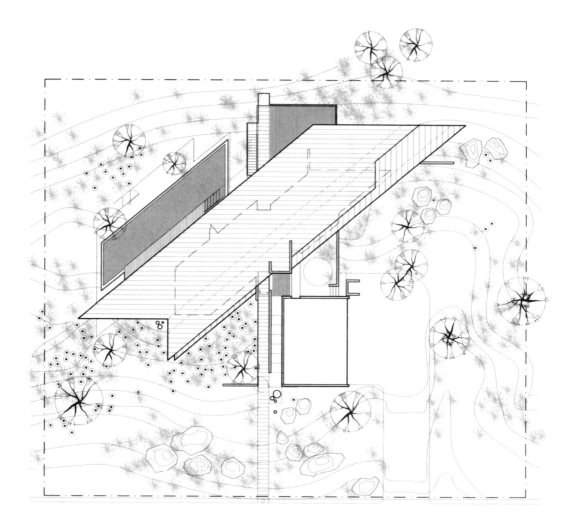

Site plan

The configuration of the dwelling —a parallelogram built on two levels— emerged in response to the natural elements of the location. Thus, the building stands between boulders and small trees, taking advantage of views of the large esplanades in the west and keeping a successful relation with the street.

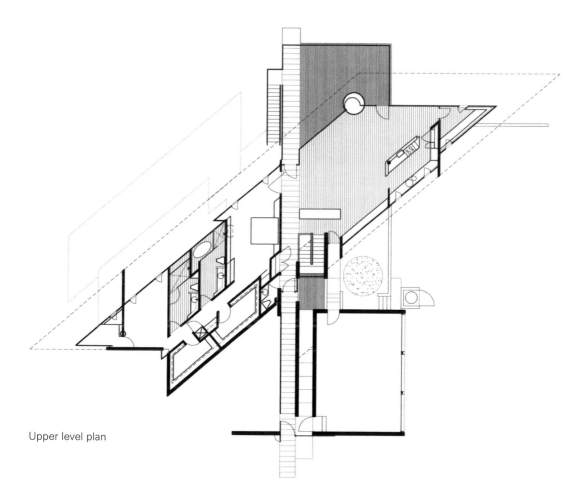

Upper level plan

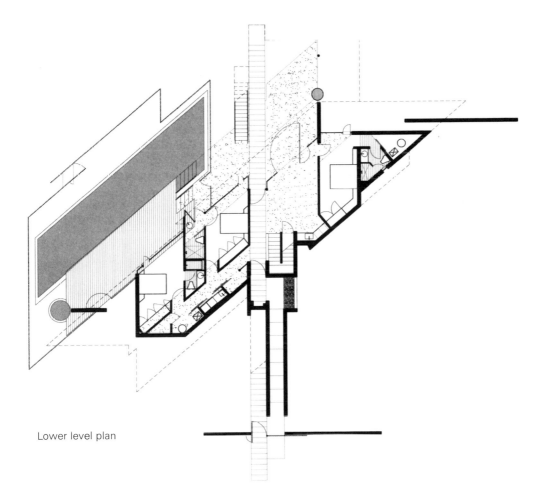

Lower level plan

Satoshi Okada Architects
Villa Man-Bow
Atami, Japan

This project is a villa located in the mountains of Atami, a famous spa resort on the Pacific Ocean, about 62 miles west of Tokyo. The plot is on a steep and rocky mountain ridge, with a grade of approximately 70 degrees, facing north to splendid views of the ocean beyond the valley down below. It is some $29^{1/2}$ feet above the front street, which, in general, makes for difficult building conditions. To make matters worse, the area is noted for strong winds, high humidity and dense fogs, as well as frequent earthquakes. In particular, the salty gales blowing up through the narrow valley from the ocean represent the greatest danger to buildings in the vicinity. The strength of these furious winds has been known to knock down walls or blow off roofs during each typhoon season.

The client wanted to build a villa which would also function as a guesthouse for weekend parties in the country. The conditions that had to be addressed were: 1) dealing with the humidity of the site; 2) ensuring the splendid view of the ocean above the tree-tops; 3) mitigating the strong winds.

In lifting the building piloti-style above the ground, the architect immediately solved some of the site's more salient problems: the building is no longer obliged to conform to the steep grade of the land, humidity emanating from the ground does not enter the house and clearer views above the tree-tops are gained.

The villa is composed of two volumes; one is an ellipsoidal sphere housing most of the home's general functions, the other is a rectangular parallelepiped solely for sleeping. Each volume is supported by 6 columns of $11^{3/4}$" in diameter, on a $11^{3/4}$ feet grid formation. As protection against the wind, the sphere faces the valley in an aerodynamic manner, while the rectangle is shielded by thick tree cover. In both, the main skeleton is steel, and the ellipsoidal cage is shaped by laminated timbers.

The exterior of the ellipsoid is entirely clad in copper plates (t=0.014"), a technique for which the project is indebted to the traditional methods of shrine carpenters in Japan. The greenish patina which will accrue over time will serve as protection against the corrosion caused by the high salt content of the seaside air.

As per the client's request, interior surfaces are all painted white. In the sphere particularly, one can experience a certain endless space through voids, as well as one's own unreliable senses for understanding space without corners. This game of perception between architectural space and the human body provides the extraordinary aspect sought by the clients.

Photographs: Hiroyuki Hirai

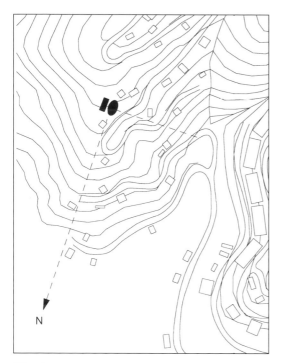

Site plan

The site is on a steep and rocky mountain ridge, with a gradient of approximately 70 degrees, facing north to a splendid view of the ocean beyond the valley down below. The villa is composed of two volumes; one is an ellipsoidal sphere for dwelling, the other is a rectangular parallelepiped solely for sleeping.

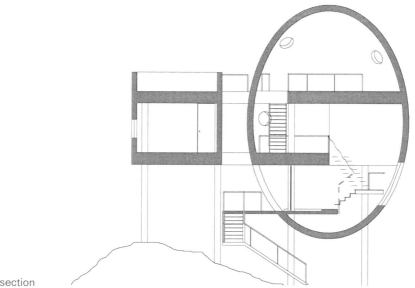

Cross section

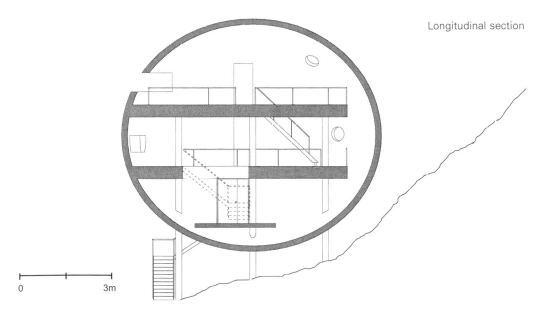

Longitudinal section

0   3m

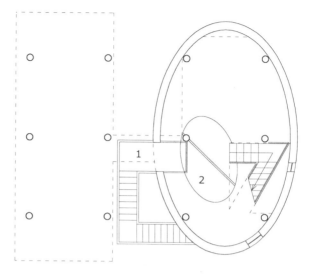

Entrance floor plan

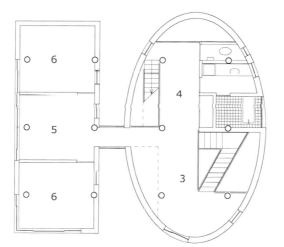

First floor plan

1. Entrance porch
2. Entrance
3. Hall
4. Gallery
5. Anteroom
6. Bedroom

The exterior of the sphere is entirely clad in copper plates, for which the project is indebted to the traditional techniques of shrine carpenters in Japan. The greenish patina which will accrue over time will serve as protection against the corrosion caused by the high salt content of the seaside air.

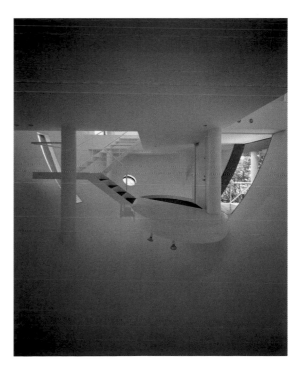

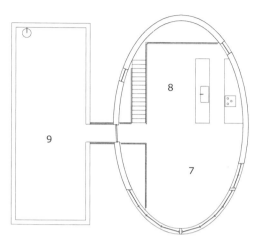

7. Living room
8. Dining room
9. Roof terrace

Second floor plan

As per the client's request, interior surfaces are all painted white. In the sphere particularly, one can experience a certain endless space through voids, as well as one's own unreliable senses for understanding space without corners. This game of perception between architectural space and the human body provides the extraordinary aspect sought by the clients.

UN Studio Van Berkel & Bos
Möbius House
Het Gooi, The Netherlands

The diagram of the double-locked torus conveys the organization of two intertwining paths, which trace how two people can live together, yet apart, meeting at certain points, which become shared spaces. The idea of two entities following their own paths while sharing certain moments, possibly also reversing roles at certain points, is extended to include the materialization of the building and its construction.

The Möbius house seamlessly integrates program, circulation and structure. The house interweaves the various states that accompany the compression of different activities into one structure: work, social and family life and individual time alone all find their places in the loop structure. Movement through this loop follows the pattern of an active day. The structure of movement is transposed onto the organization of the two main materials used for the house; glass and concrete move in front of each other and switch places. Concrete construction becomes furniture and glass facades turn into interior partition walls.

As a graphic representation of 24 hours of family life, the diagram acquires a time-space dimension, which leads to the implementation of the Möbius band.

Equally the site and its relationship to the building are important for the design. The site covers two hectares, which are divided into four areas, each with its own distinct character. Linking these with the internal organization of the Möbius band transforms living in the house into a walk in the landscape.

The mathematical model of the Möbius is not literally transferred to the building, but is conceptualized or thematicized and can be found in architectural ingredients, such as the light and staircases and the way in which people move through the house. So, while the Möbius diagram introduces aspects of duration and trajectory, the diagram is worked into the building in a mutated way.

The instrumentalization of this simple drawing is the key. The two interlocking lines are suggestive of the formal organization of the building, but that is only the beginning; diagrammatic architecture is a process of unfolding and ultimately of liberation.

Photographs: Christian Richters

The design concept for this dwelling is based on the Möbius band. This construction reflects the two entwined paths which allow the cohabitation of its two inhabitants without losing their privacy.

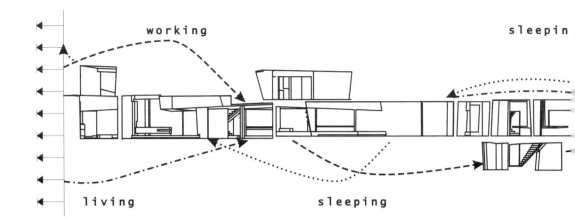

working

sleepin

living

sleeping

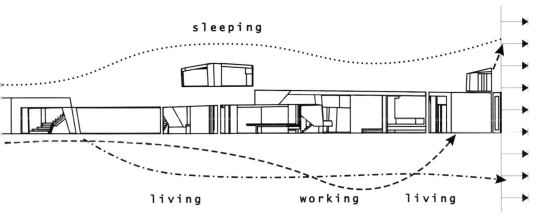

sleeping

living   working   living

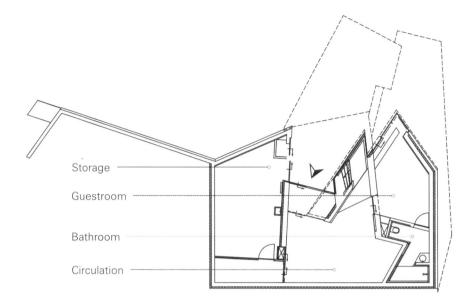

Storage

Guestroom

Bathroom

Circulation

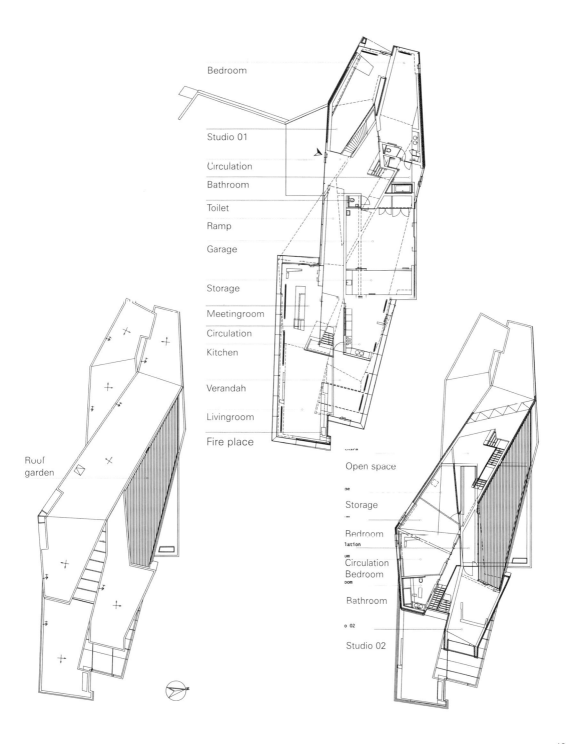

Bedroom

Studio 01

Circulation

Bathroom

Toilet

Ramp

Garage

Storage

Meetingroom

Circulation

Kitchen

Verandah

Livingroom

Fire place

Roof
garden

Open space

ae

Storage

Bedroom
lation

um
Circulation
Bedroom
oom

Bathroom

o 02

Studio 02

The distribution of the dwelling's various interior settings follows no linear or compartmentalizing criteria; rather it has been conceived as a continuum where the spaces easily interrelate.

Niall McLaughlin
Northamptonshire Shack
Northamptonshire, UK

This dwelling is located on agricultural land that was used as a reconnaissance base by the allied forces during WWII. The building was constructed manually, without any working drawings and in conjunction with a landscape scheme, so in its development the modifications were open to all those involved.

The client, a photographer specialized in insects and nature with back lighting and special effects, wanted a house that also served as a setting for his work. He therefore decided to regenerate an abandoned pond that was lost amidst a labyrinth of brambles and bushes.

After the water had been filtered and oxygenated with plants, the brambles and bushes had been cleared away and the water had been populated with fish, the pond recovered its life and could attract the dragonflies and other animals that would be used as models for the photographer.

The form and the materials of the building were conceived with the intention of capturing and storing several types of light. Some external spaces, such as the south area giving onto the pond, are used as rooms in which objects could be placed for photographing under the required conditions. A long arm was also built over the pond to photograph insects on the surface with the water as a background. To take advantage of the geographical situation of this dwelling, the architect incorporated a sauna, a bedroom and a belvedere with views over the aquatic landscape and the surrounding grasslands.

The building combines wood, masonry, metal cladding and other elements, and a fiber-glass wing whose extended staircases of polycarbonate and perforated metal emerge from the water. Due to the curious external appearance, the access to the dwelling is like the entrance to a hidden cave.

The main elements of the structure are the numerous "wing" elements that crawl over the rear part of the building, the skylight that runs along the longitudinal axis, and a complex overhanging roof supported by fine metal angles laid out in a fan-shape that bend with the force of the strong wind that blows in this area.

Photographs: Nicholas Kane

144

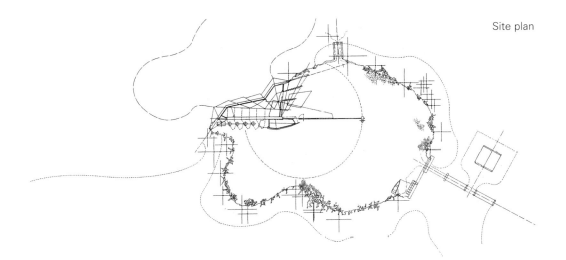

The effects of light on the exterior are supplemented inside the dwelling by means of the incorporation of polycarbonate deflectors on the roof, just above the skylight. These are secured by fine rods that diffuse the rays of light creating a pleasant illumination.

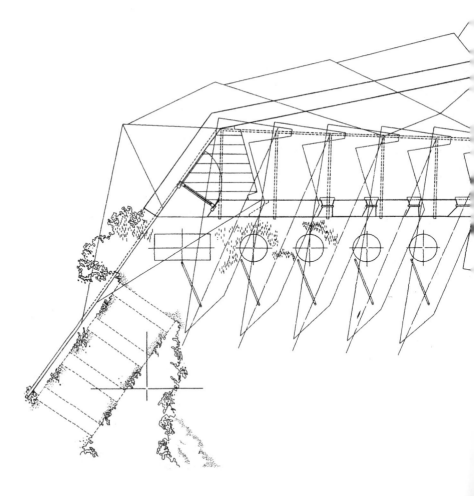

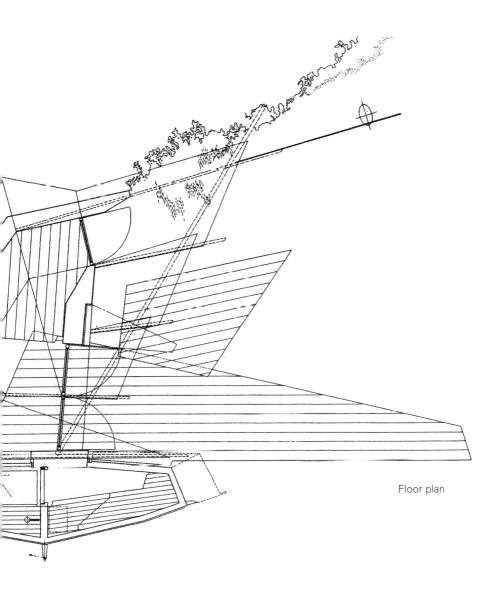

Floor plan

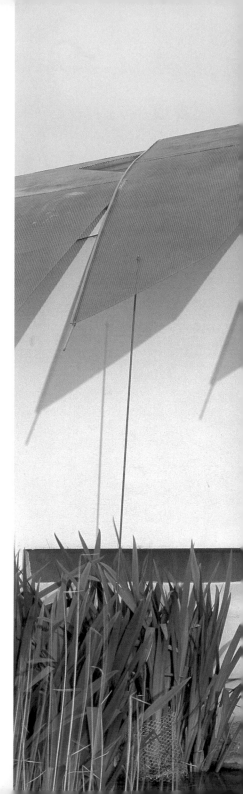

Jo Crepain Architect NV
Water Tower
Brasschaat, Belgium

Until 1937, this water tower with a height of over 75$\frac{1}{2}$ ft was used to provide water to the castle and other buildings of the county of Brasschaat, near the city of Antwerp. After being in disuse for decades due to the construction of four new water tanks and the planning of a modern water supply system, it survived a planned demolition. The conservation of this peculiar cylindrical tower crowned by a large, four-meter-high cistern allowed it to be converted into an unusual single-family dwelling. The architect respected the original industrial typology, leaving the four large pillars that sustain the structure exposed, and also maintained the compositional structure and the essential functionality of the original design. This was achieved by minimizing the presence of decorative objects and by limiting the elements and materials to reinforced concrete, structural glass and galvanized metal.

Around the original structure, a parallelepiped, double-height volume with a mezzanine surrounds the tower at ground level. This new construction houses the services and a living room that is totally open and transparent to the exterior. This breaks the verticality of the scheme and gains space, and its roof acts as a terrace for the first floor, which houses the main bedroom.

The new tower achieves its maximum expressiveness when it is illuminated at night. The transparency of the glass structure that wraps the building allows the occupants to enjoy the wooded landscape with a small winding creek and reveals the three floors of 13x13 ft, each with a small balcony. These floors house, from bottom to top, the study, the guest bedroom and a small winter garden. At the top of the tower the water cistern is conserved, now transformed into a curious windowless space that is intended for private receptions.

Photographs: Sven Everaert/Ludo Noël

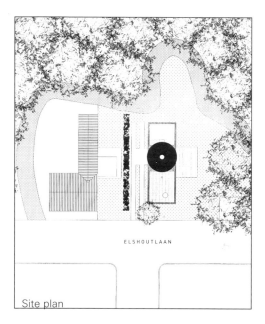

ELSHOUTLAAN

Site plan

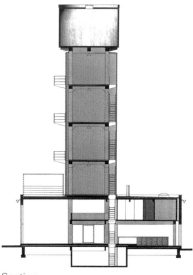

Section

154

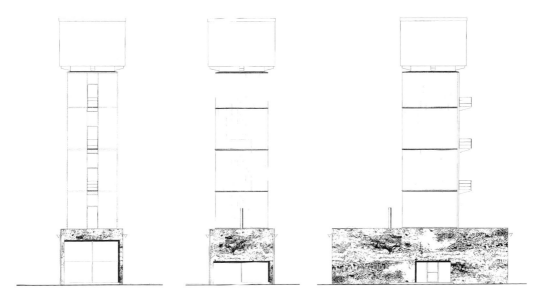

From the front, this old water tower has a very similar appearance to that of the original building. At first sight, the glass and galvanized metal seem to be the only additions to the structure.

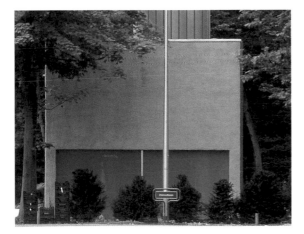

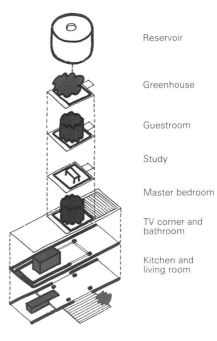

Reservoir

Greenhouse

Guestroom

Study

Master bedroom

TV corner and bathroom

Kitchen and living room

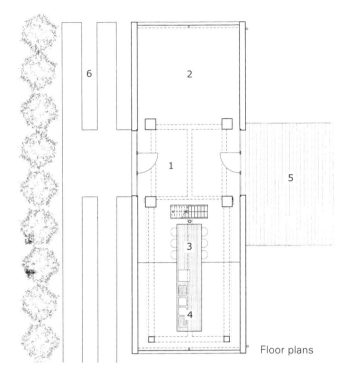

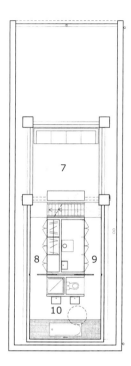

Floor plans

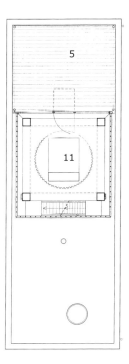

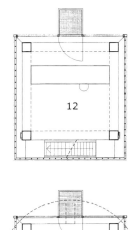

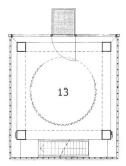

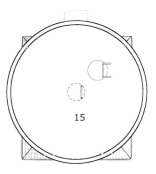

1. Entrance
2. Living-room
3. Dining
4. Kitchen
5. Terrace

6. Garage
7. TV-corner
8. Dressing
9. Storage
10. Bathroom

11. Bedroom
12. Study
13. Guestroom
14. Winter garden
15. Water tank

The construction of a larger volume on the first two floors, in which all the communal areas and services are housed, breaks the spatial limitation of the rest of the floors and is the most striking feature of the tower.

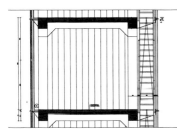

Section XX

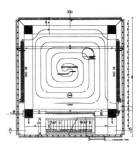

Section YY

Floor plan

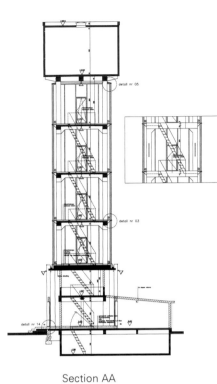

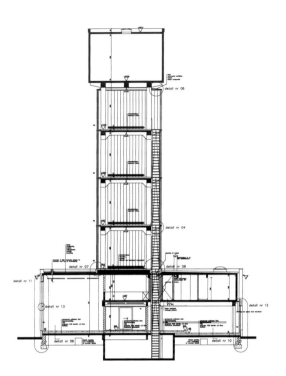

Section AA

Section BB

160

Brookes Stacey Randall
Lowe Apartment
London, UK

Brookes Stacey Randall were appointed by Chris Lowe of the Pet Shop Boys to provide a "calm light interior space" within the top floor of a converted warehouse.

The form of the existing shell was a very particular half arch with a small side space. A potential roof terrace was separated from the main volume and accessed via a lower terrace and spiral staircase.

The main volume was treated as a room whose function can change depending on the particular facilities brought into use. In order to achieve this, the small side space was split into storage and bathroom areas. The storage area was equipped with three large pull-out 'pods', each providing a different facility for the main space. Each pod was designed to cantilever out on a triple extending mechanism, similar in principal to that of a filing cabinet drawer.

Directly above the center of the space, a curved double glazed rooflight opens on hydraulic arms. Light is controlled by automatic pivoting aluminum louvers. The lighting concept was developed to enhance the architecture rather than simply light the space. The window screens are both lit from behind to allow a gentle transition from day to night.

Daylight is modified through a combination of translucent screens and opaque blind and louvers allowing the client total control over the degree of privacy and light.

The circulation within the flat has been designed to maximize a sense of scale, concealing views and revealing them as the user moves through the space. The convergent curved walls lead the user from the dim entrance toward the light of the main space whilst the route broadens and the height increases towards the curved ceiling rising above. A slatted birch mezzanine closes over the route. From the position below the mezzanine, the kitchen and dining areas are revealed to the rear and the full space opens up towards the birch screens on the end window.

Photographs: Katsuhisha Kida

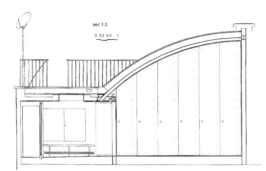

sec 1.2

0 0.2 0.5 1

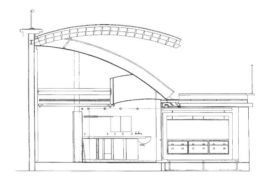

Cross sections

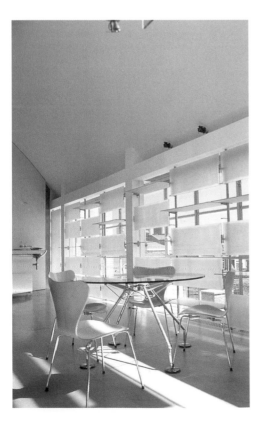

Axonometric view

The staircase built totally in structurally resistant glass is designed to be as light and transparent as possible to avoid interrupting the visual continuity of the space.

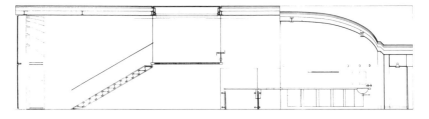

Longitudinal section

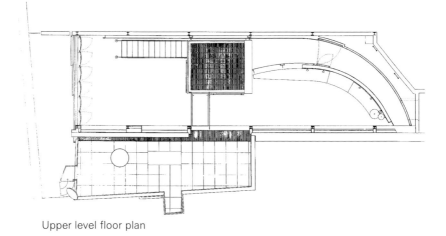

Upper level floor plan

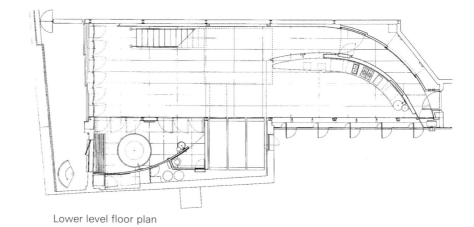

Lower level floor plan

In the bathroom the architects used a fiber optic lighting system that is able to fill the space with light thanks to its reflection on the multiple stainless steel surfaces.

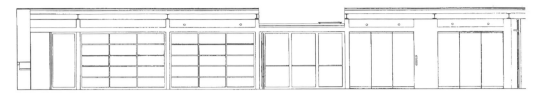

Interior elevation

The existing space is divided into two areas of different heights, one of which is covered with a half arch.

Three large sliding fitted cupboards are pulled out to modify the large space according to the user's needs.

171

Bart Prince
Gradow Family Residence
Aspen, Colorado, USA
Hight Residence
Mendocino, California, USA

Bart Prince's project for the Gradow family in Aspen, Colorado, is on a large site (40 acres) with spectacular views in all directions. The clients wanted to see these views from every room; thus, the design climbs the hill in steps, each grouping of spaces looking out over those below. The main entry is on an upper level, from which there is access, either via a long stairway-gallery or via elevator, to the large living area below, bounded on one side by a curving frameless glass wall overlooking the mountains and valleys. Above this are four structures which mount the hill progressively. From the bottom up, the various levels contain: the master bedroom suite; the children's bedrooms and guest quarters; the offices and staff areas with photography lab; and finally, the gym and lap pools. The translucent side walls of the lap pool space slide open in good weather to completely expose the distant views down the mountain.

The Hight Residence is on a beautiful two-acre site on the cliffs overlooking the Pacific Ocean near the town of Mendocino, California. It is designed to function initially as a holiday or weekend home, but will become the owner's main residence in a few years. It is sited to take advantage of the views to the south and southwest, while shielding the occupants from the near constant winds form the north.

On the ground floor, the house is divided at the entry by a breezeway, which separates the garage with guestroom above from the main living areas and other bedrooms. The cedar-shingled, glu-laminated undulating roof divides at this entry point to allow the visitor to take cover from the wind and rain and yet see right through the structure to the sea and rock islands beyond.

Photographs: Robert Reck, Barbi Benton, Bart Prince

Gradow Family Residence

The house cascades down the mountainside in a series of fan-shaped volumes affording panoramic views.

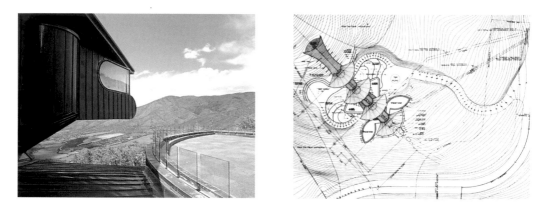

Site plan

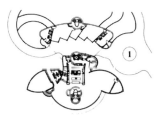 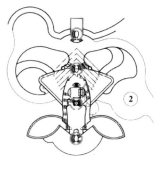 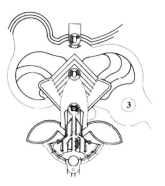

1. Living, kitchen
2. Dining, entrance, terraces

3. Master bedroom
4. Guest bedroom, Children's bedroom

5. Offices, dark room
6. Gym, swimming pool

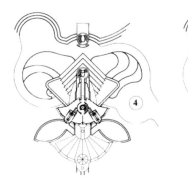 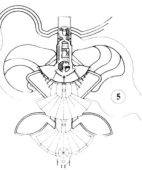 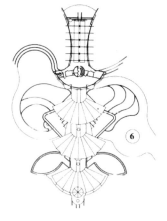

Succession of plans from top to bottom

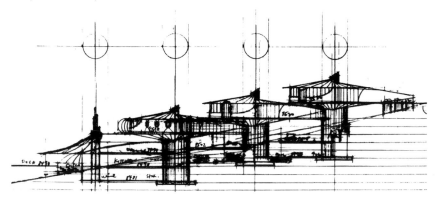

Although its form adapts to the terrain, the house integrates into the landscape by contraposition, particularly in fine weather when the reflection of the extensive surfaces of glass and copper cuts a powerful silhouette.

The combination of materials is quite unusual. The exterior finish of the "pod" structure is copper and glass. The structural system is steel frame with wood frame infill supported on reinforced concrete and masonry service cores which contain the stairs, elevator and mechanical and electrical equipment.

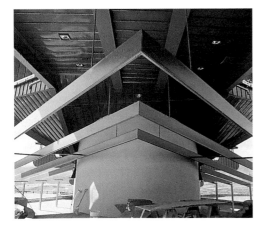

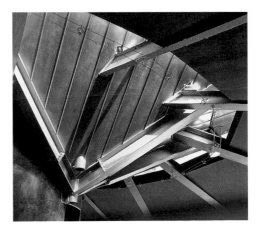

Hight Residence

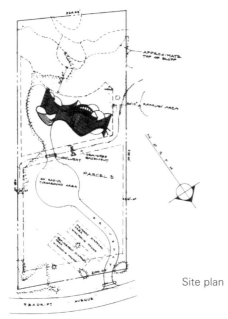

Site plan

The structure is not simply a frame, on which the architecture rests but is rather an integral part of the design. The spaces are generated on the basis of the internal structure and are expressed in the external appearance. On the north side, the roof reaches the ground to guide the wind over the house, whereas the south side is open, with terraces overlooking the best views.

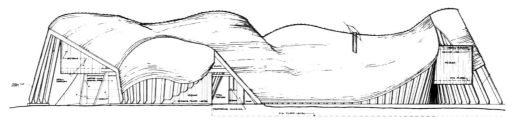

EAST ELEVATION

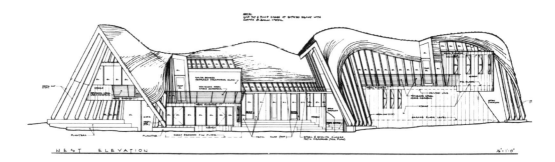

WEST ELEVATION

179

Ground floor plan

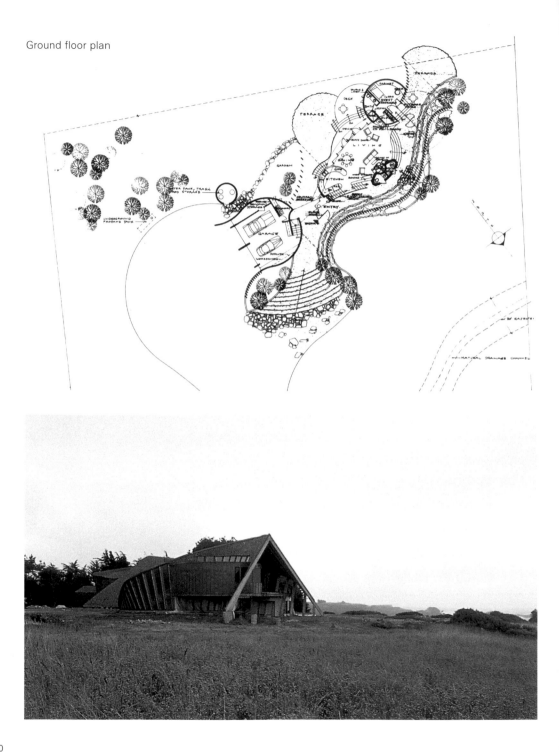

Upper floor plan

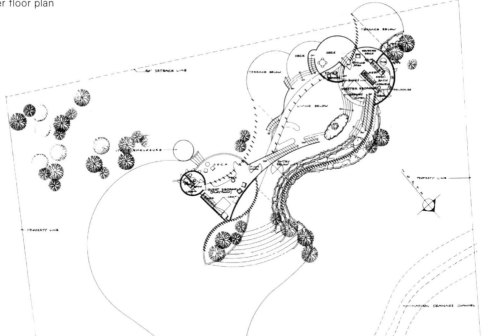

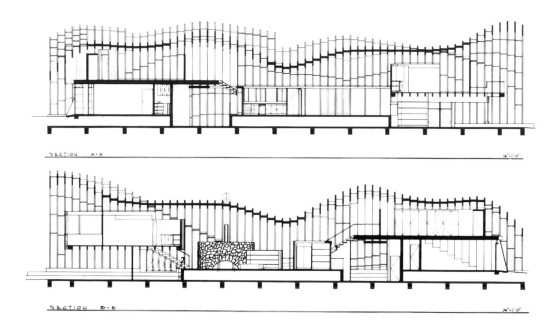

SECTION A·A   ¼"·1'·0"

SECTION B·B   ¼"·1'·0"

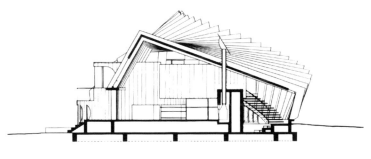

SECTION C·C   ¼"·1'·0"

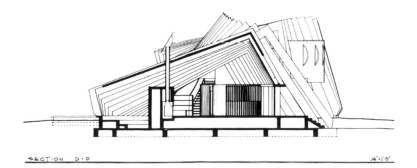

SECTION D·D   ¼"·1'·0"

The roof structure is visible from inside as a series of glu-laminated beams which create an undulating surface of wood, copper and glass forming a large space visible from one end to the other over partitions of the bedrooms.

Waro Kishi & K. Associates
House in Shimogamo
Kyoto, Japan

This two story house is located in an urban area at the foot of the Kitayama mountains in the northern part of Kyoto. Covering almost the entire plot, the house has a frontage of 10$^{1/2}$ feet x 18" and a depth of 13 feet x 27". At the core of the steel-frame structure, the architect has created a nakaniwa (inner court) measuring 6$^{1/2}$ feet x 27". The rest of the house consists of a steel frame with exterior walls made of formed cement plates, steel sashes, and large doors.

Designing this house, Kishi was fully aware that the contemporary urban house can only convey a sense of reality as a one-off solution to a number of fixed preconditions. Simultaneously, though, he attempted to create a kind of urban house prototype, a dream of 20th century modernism. He thus focused on incorporating new ideas into planning and structure.

In designing the house, the main intention was not to secure privacy. Instead, the architect placed emphasis on the relationship between the exterior space –that is, the nakaniwa- and the rooms facing it. The result is a large one-room living space, with individual rooms that are independent yet mutually interrelated.

Nor was preference given to the structure. Rather, it was understood as a part of the over-all assembly of basic elements, in order to achieve the impression of a single functional unit. After all, several decades after the mythological age of modern architecture the time may have come to re-think architecture in the age of technology.

Photographs: Hiroyuki Hirai

The three-dimensional structure, treated as just another element of the building, gives unity to the functional units of the dwelling.

The dwelling relates to the outdoor space through an inner court situated in the core of the steel structure. The inner court gives access to the dwelling and becomes the heart of the scheme, with all the rooms looking out onto it.

Alfons Soldevila
Translucent House
Barcelona, Spain

This experimental house is a prototype for a dwelling done by the students at the School of Architecture of Barcelona, under the tutelage of Alfons Soldevila. In making full use of natural resources for achieving light, heat and ventilation, the "translucent house" displays optimal qualities of comfort and spatial design considerations.

With a rectangular floor plan and curved roof, the house takes maximum advantage of sunlight, which can be guided to different areas.

The walls, slabs and roof are translucent, thereby aiding in the ample distribution of light -as well as the varying effects produced by its passage through policarbonate panels- throughout the space.

Of equal importance are the effects of natural light on the interior of the home, as well as those brought about on the exterior with the nighttime projection of artificial lighting emanating from the interior.

The distribution of the different floor slabs creates a highly flexible space. Thus, the interior of the house can be distributed as seen fit. The façade has a single opening (of 19$\frac{3}{4}$ feet), which provides quick and effective ventilation, aided by the openings on the upper level. Furthermore, if any particular view is of special interest, the building's flexibility makes it possible to install windows wherever needed.

On the basis of studied calculations, the construction system has been designed to make it possible for just one person to build it.

Finally, this experimental dwelling prototype is in tune with the projects on which Alfons Soldevila habitually works, always taking the material possibilities to an extreme and achieving high quality design results, while setting precedents in projects of this kind.

Photographs: Alfons Soldevila &
               ETSAB's students

The shape of the house maximizes the use of sunlight, which can be oriented as desired. This dwelling, with its rectangular floor plan and curved roof, is made up of three stepped floors, which are separated from the ground. A lengthwise stairway interconnects these floors. This is a conventional platform placement that could be modified, introducing intermediate platforms and thereby changing the layout of the interior space.

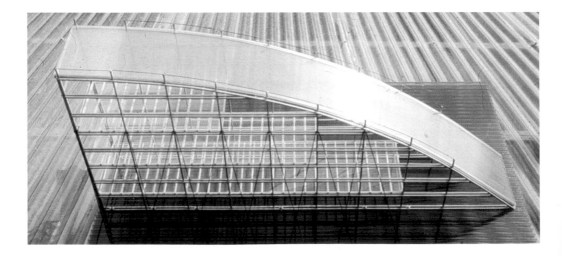

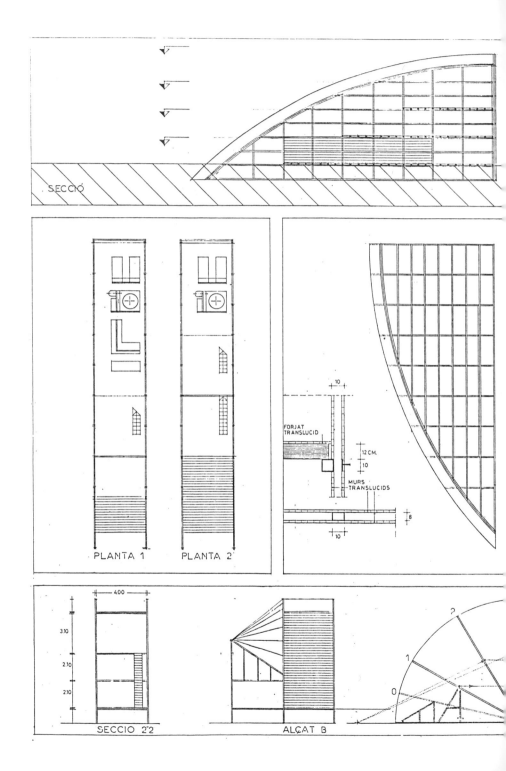

SECCIÓ

FORJAT
TRANSLUCID

12 CM.

MURS
TRANSLUCIDS

10

10

10

8

PLANTA 1   PLANTA 2

4.00

3.10

2.10

2.10

SECCIO 2'2   ALÇAT B

2

1

0

194

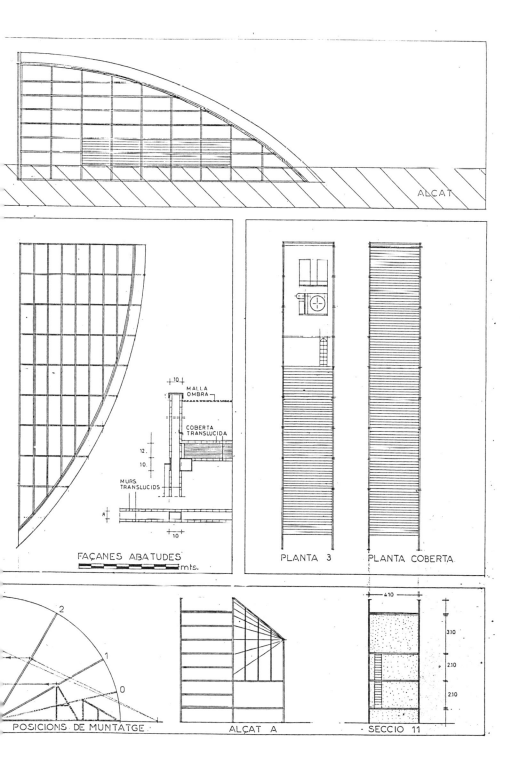

ALÇAT

FAÇANES ABATUDES

MALLA OMBRA

COBERTA TRANSLUCIDA

MURS TRANSLUCIDS

PLANTA 3   PLANTA COBERTA

POSICIONS DE MUNTATGE   ALÇAT A   SECCIO 11

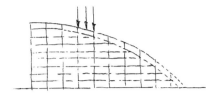

Rain

Rainwater can be channelled into a small well located at the lower end of the roof, and re-used for other purposes, such as watering plants.

Air

All of the warm air in the house ends up on the upper floor, from where it can easily be expelled to the exterior. In the winter, warm air can be recycled via a tube with a fan or "plenum" and thus fed into the lower portion of the first slab.

Light

The ground floor lighting has been filtered through various planes. The light entering from the roof reaches the lower floor after having passed through two horizontal planes. Thus, the ground floor receives direct light from the façade as well as from the upper levels, where it is also filtered by the slabs.

Cleaning

The finishes and materials used in the interior are exactly the same as those on the exterior. Therefore, water can be used for cleaning throughout the interior, even in the closets, which are of transparent plastic with a zipper.

Ventilation

Hot air rises to the upper levels. In the winter, it can be recycled and, in summertime, it is expelled via a large opening: one meter high, four meters wide. By removing a number of 3" strips from the lower levels, good ventilation can be achieved.

Solar Protection

Keeping the building from heating up in the summer could be a problem. To prevent this, the structure has been equipped with wire mesh, which is separated by 23½" and attached to the top of the porticos.

Construction details

The characteristics of the house -with a striking treatment of translucency and visual lightness- make unconventional solutions and a divergence from the norm possible.

These photos show the effects of the luminosity of the interior on the structure's surroundings.

Kei'ichi Irie
T House
Tokyo, Japan

This house was built in a residential area in central Tokyo. Two separate households live on the first floor, and a family with four members resides on the second and third floors. The introduction of multi-dimensional analysis into the architectural structure has instantly expanded the possibilities of overall views.

Many features of this T House are indebted to engineering in structural design: the option of arranging a huge top-light or thin pillars without any restrictions; floors hollowed out in cylindrical shape; and beamless slabs. Here, state-of-the-art technology is probably at its best, attributing an unpretentious view of the end result.

The overall composition, based on a simple arrangement of a circle and a square, consists of three elements: floors carved out by freely positioned skylights and cylinders, 15 slender columns (10"), and a flat slab (10"). The structure was determined through multi-dimensional analysis. Composed of rectangles and the circles of the cylinders, the second and third floors are partitioned by large sliding doors, but are fundamentally horizontally and vertically continuous; the overall space is understood as one fluidly connected space. Inside the space there is a cylinder (bathroom) and a cube (sanitary room). The first floor is treated as a base, partly composed of piloti, and is painted in monochrome (yellow), unlike the upper floors.

Photographs: Hiroyuki Hirai

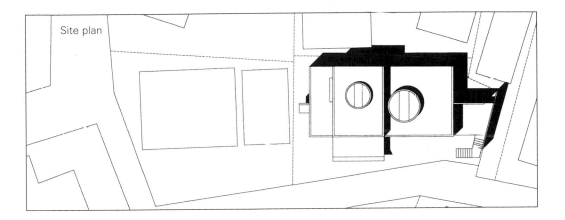

Site plan

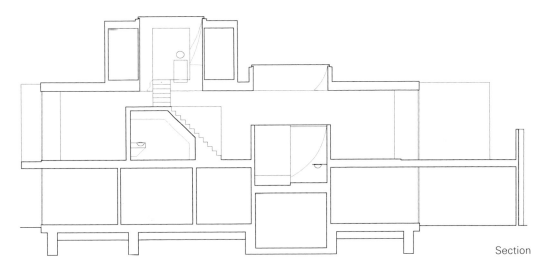

Section

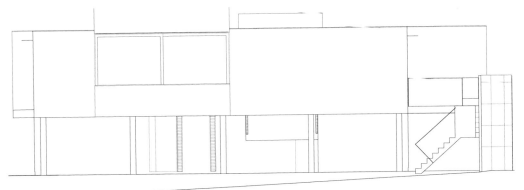

West elevation

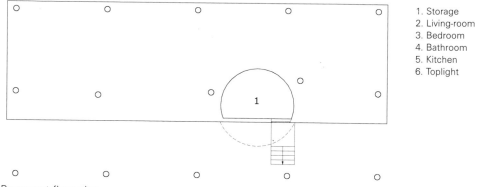

1. Storage
2. Living-room
3. Bedroom
4. Bathroom
5. Kitchen
6. Toplight

Basement floor plan

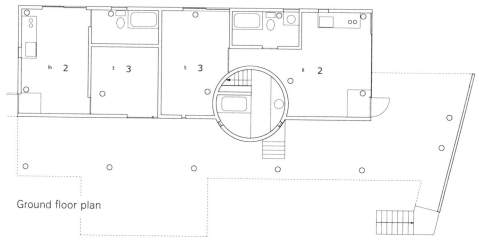
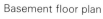

Ground floor plan

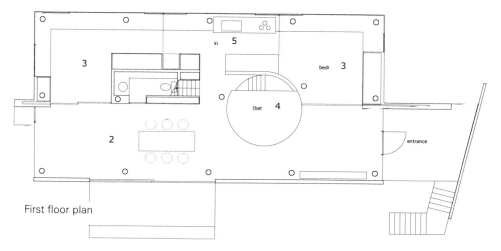

First floor plan

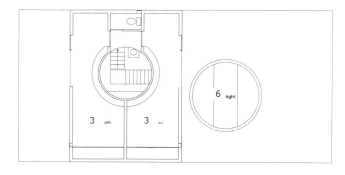

The house consists of a simple arrangement of a circle and a square. Sliding doors offer flexibility in spatial divisions, maintaining continuity both horizontally and vertically.

Second floor plan

The spaces of the dwelling are defined by geometric and chromatic elements. The use of three basic colors —black, red and white— and the predominance of elementary forms —the square and the circle— organize the distribution of the space and create different atmospheres inside the building.

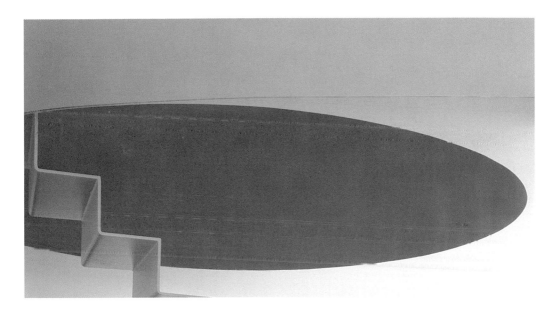

Oswald Mathias Ungers
Wasserturm
Utscheid, Germany

The original tower dating from 1957 had only the two upper floors, housing the water tank and machinery, and a high entrance hall. The kitchen floor is a new addition, and is overlooked by a gallery running parallel to the stairs. On the first level is a newly constructed element containing the bedroom with shower, bath and fitted cupboards. The top floor is a tall space with four windows: sparsely furnished, it is a meditation area with breathtaking views over the Eifel Mountains. As one enters the tower one is struck by the succession of spaces that have been created: the alternation of wide-narrow and high-low. Emerging from the low, narrow stairwell there is always a high, wide space with a view of the landscape. The spaces in the water tower are simple elements stacked one on top of the other, but the art of the design lay in adapting and refining the existing aesthetics to the new use. The spaces and materials are thus left in their purest form: sandstone, the circular form of the steps, the verticality of the layout, the new additions — all is pure, unobtrusive, natural.

An example of this is that the windows largely follow the original design, serving less an idea of living space and views, and more the original purpose of illumination: one window on the stairwell, one in the kitchen and one in the bathroom. However, on the second floor the situation is different. Four windows point in the direction of the four cardinal points, thus adding a new dimension to the circular plan thanks to the conceptual rigor of the architect, who pursued the maxim "Less is more" with laudable sensitivity.

Photographs: Stefan Müller

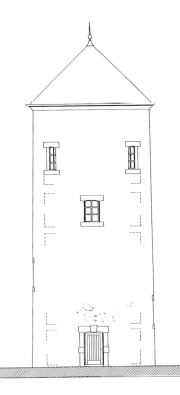

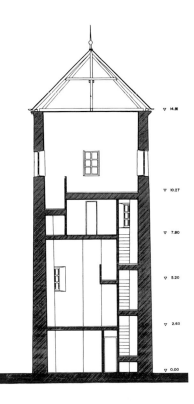

Main façade

Cross section

The kitchen is located on the ground floor. The photograph shows two of the four interior columns that stabilize the thick sandstone walls and function as totally independent elements.

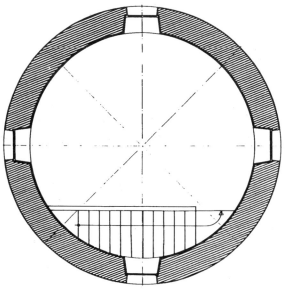

Third floor plan

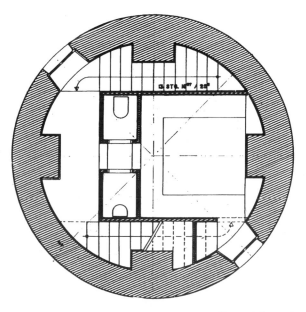

Second floor plan

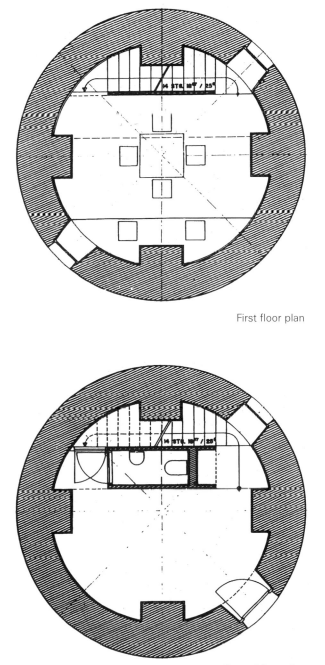

First floor plan

Ground floor plan

The project made use of the building's existing openings; except on the top floor, where four new windows face the four cardinal points.

Michael Jantzen
M-House
Gorman, California, USA

Relocatable M-vironments are made of a wide variety of manipulatable components that can be connected in many different ways to a matrix of modular support frames. The frames can be assembled and disassembled in different ways to accommodate a wide range of changing needs.

The M-house, which is made from the M-vironmens system, consists of a series of rectangular panels that are attached with hinges to an open space frame grid of seven interlocking cubes. The panels are hinged to the cubes in either a horizontal or a vertical orientation. The hinges allow the panels to fold into or out of the cube frames to perform various functions.

Some of the panels are insulated and contain windows and doors. These panels can completely enclose spaces that are heated and cooled. Other un-insulated panels fold in or out, over and around these open platforms.

The platforms and the cube frames are supported by adjustable legs which are attached to load-bearing footpads. In many cases the support frames do not require a foundation, and they can be adjusted to accommodate terrain variations.

All of the M-House components are interchangeable, and can be increased or decreased in number and size. The panels can be made in a curved configuration and from many different types of materials.

The existing M-house was designed to function as a single private vacation retreat, or in multiple configurations, as a complete stand-alone, high-tech resort complex.

The house can be designed to be self sufficient, powered by alternative energy sources such as the sun and wind. With different sizes, shapes, materials, and panel types, the system can be used for exhibits, pavilions, play environments for kids, retail spaces, office modules, and many other commercial applications.

Photographs: Michael Jantzen

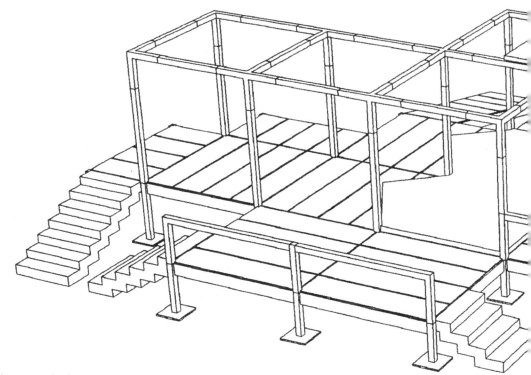

Axonometric view

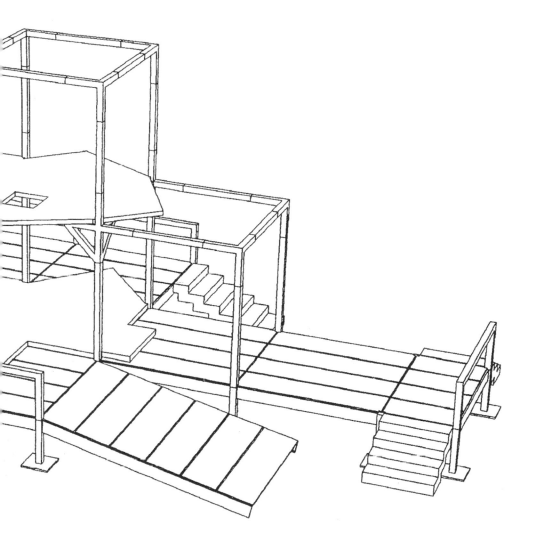

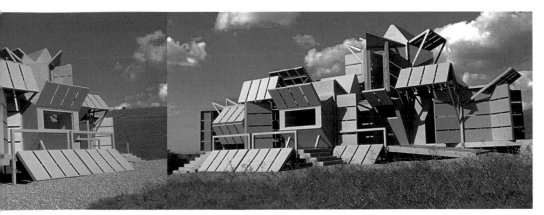

Axonometric view

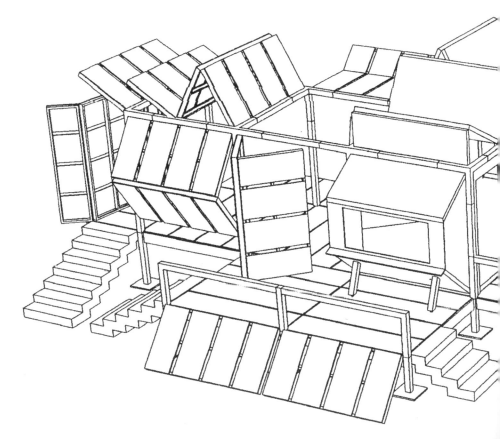

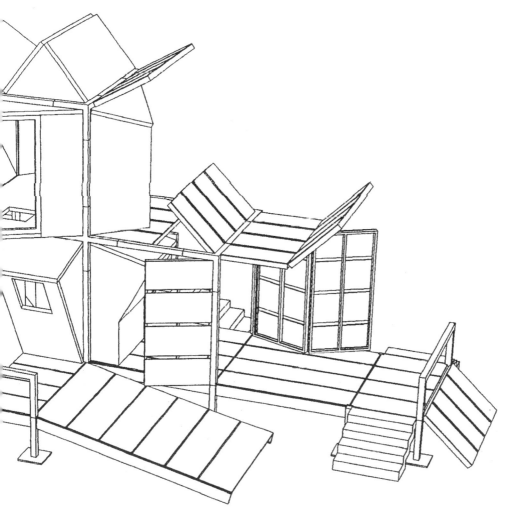

Thanks to the system of folding panels, the dwelling can be opened or closed to regulate the temperature of the interior. The spaces created also have optimum natural lighting thanks to the strategic arrangement of windows and skylights.

Floor plan

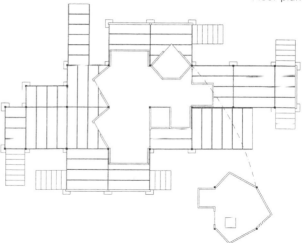

Shigeru Ban
Paper House
Yamanakako, Japan

Shigeru Ban, one of the most innovative architects of recent time, has been studying the characteristics of paper as a building element since the '80s Though there is some resistance to its use in a structural system, paper is a material that may be treated —like wood— to make it resistant to fire, water and damp. It is also easy to recycle and economic, factors which allowed the architect to work with this element in designs that required speed and low cost, such as the pavilions for refugees from Rwanda and the provisional buildings to house the victims of the Kobe earthquake.

In this scheme (a dwelling of 1.184 ft^2) the structure is formed by two square horizontal planes with a side of 32$^{3/4}$ feet and paper tubes aligned in an S-shape with a height of 9 feet, a diameter of 11" and a thickness of 0.6". These tubes support the house and define its functional spaces, relating them to the surrounding landscape. Ten of these tubes support the vertical loads and eighty interior tubes support the lateral loads. The circle formed by these eighty tubes defines the living room, whereas the circle formed by the square defines the bathroom of the dwelling.

The separation from the exterior is created using a glass wall that may open or close and that can also be covered by canvas curtains to provide privacy and good insulation. The spatial continuity between the interior and the landscape is achieved through the horizontal elements and the use of highly diaphanous joinery, and through the definition of the interior spaces with the minimum number of elements, following the example of the great architects of Modernism.

The paper tubes also allow the spaces defined to maintain a very subtle relation with the surrounding spaces, letting in light and views between them.

Photographs: Hiroyuki Hirai

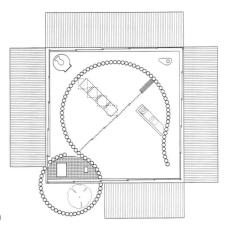

Floor plan

Axonometric view

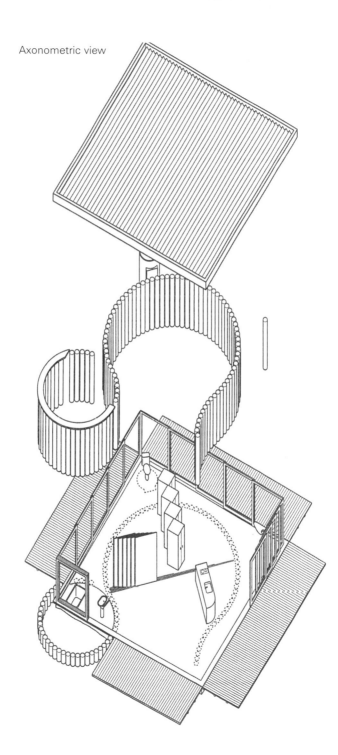

Cross section

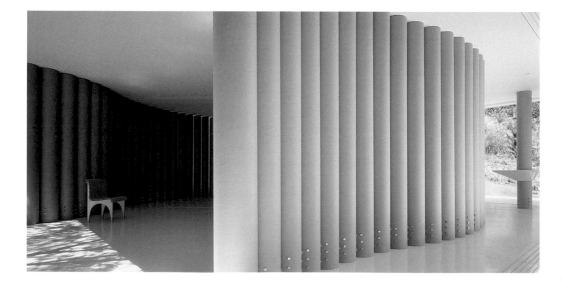

The relation between the interior and exterior spaces is a constant in the designs of Shigeru Ban. In this scheme, the enormous glazed window can be opened to leave the dwelling totally open to the exterior. To emphasize this relation even further, it was decided to create overhanging terraces that extend the floor area and bring the dwelling closer to nature.

José Gigante
Wind Mill Reconversion
Vilar de Mouros, Caminha, Portugal

On the grounds of a restored house in northern Portugal, an old abandoned windmill waited its turn to be put back into use. In the course of time the idea finally arose of transforming this peculiar building into a small auxiliary dwelling belonging to the main house, giving it its own life and thus creating a completely inhabitable and independent space that could be used as a place of rest. For José Gigante, the architect in charge of the conversion, the presence of the mill was so strong that any major intervention would have minimized its charm. Therefore, without touching any of the thick granite walls, an unusual copper roof with a very gentle slope was added.

The intention was to respect the memory of the place as far as possible, so the inspiration for the transformation began naturally from the inside towards the outside.

The layout and organization of the small space, with only eight square metres per floor, was not easy. Thanks to the choice of wood as the main building material, a welcoming atmosphere enhanced by the curved walls and the minimum number of openings was achieved.

On the lower floor, a large rock acts as an entrance step. On this level, a minimal space was sought where a number of different activities could be carried out. It houses a bathroom and a living room, with the possibility of transforming a small sofa into a curious bed: it is conceived as a case that contains all the necessary pieces for assembling the bed. On the upper floor, the furnishings are limited to a cupboard and a table/bed that is extended to the window.

The only openings are those that already existed in the mill and they have been left as they were conceived, with their natural capacity to reveal the exterior and to illuminate a space in which the contrasts between the materials cannot be ignored.

The typology of this building was crucial to the restorations to which it has been subjected, and shows why the interior space is so important in this scheme. The thick circular walls occupy more space than the interior of the mill, but they hug the whole room and provide a welcoming and unconventional sensation that give this building a new and innovative perspective.

Photographs: Luís Ferreira Alves

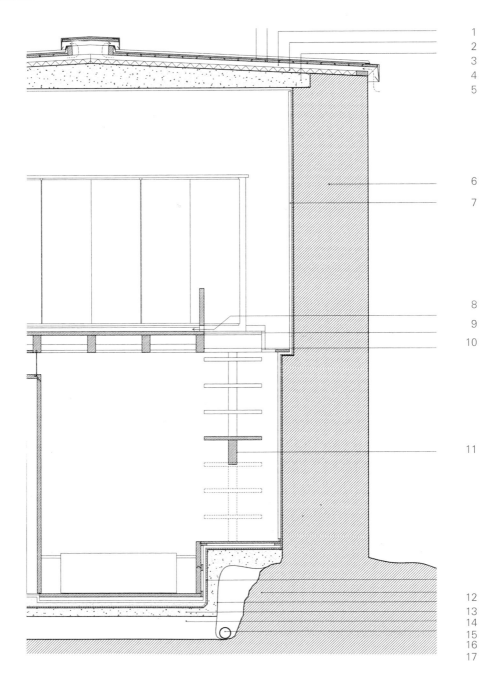

1
2
3
4
5

6
7

8
9
10

11

12
13
14
15
16
17

1. Copper cladding
2. Pine platform
3. Air chamber
4. Thermal insulation
5. Reinforced concrete panel
6. Existing granite masonry
7. Render
8. Air chamber
9. Beech wood floor
10. Beech wood frame
11. Beech wood staircase
12. Waterproof mortar
13. Existing rocky dike
14. Geotextile
15. Concrete wall
16. Gravel box
17. Pipe

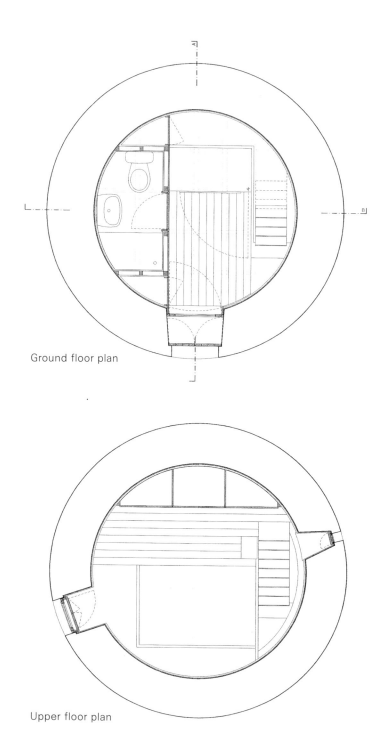

Ground floor plan

Upper floor plan

The choice of wood as the main construction element in the rehabilitation, in perfect combination with the white curved walls, creates a calm and welcoming atmosphere.

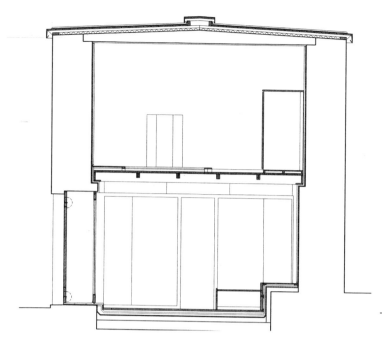

Cross sections

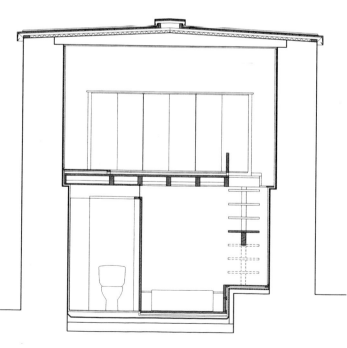

The use of wood and the maximum use of space are the main characteristics of this scheme. To solve the problem of the lack of space, a system was devised in which a bed is hidden at the foot of the staircase.

Kister Scheithauer Gross
Mach House
Dessau-Mosigkau, Germany

The building is designed as a single-family home with an integrated fully separate apartment. It has a total residential floor area of approx. 588 (390+168) feet and is based on an ecological energy-use concept making it almost autonomous in terms of external power needs.

A determining design factor was the location of the building. The site had been originally occupied by a market gardening operation. Starting out from an ecological low-energy concept that was to be reflected in the projected building character, greenhouse building traditions were decided upon.

A rural building approach has been adopted, but interpreting it as a technically innovative residential building which exercises a pilot function in its present configuration.

To an approaching observer, the façade is a decorative concrete wall with a large wooden gate, behind which an arrangement of interior yards divide the access wall and the actual building. As a result, the house retains a discreet presence when viewed from the road, remaining concealed behind trees and opening outward to visitors via a sequence of paths that take them across an array of patios and yards.

The inner building core is formed by two load-bearing concrete walls with a stiffening function which also serve as decorative concrete surfaces. Comprised between them is the central corridor on the ground floor and the central technical room arranged on the upper level.

The exterior building front consists of a structure of glue laminated timber uprights with Betoplan (cpoxy coated plywood) panel bracing. The panels are fixed, with reddish shadow joints for contrast, or provided in the form of movable wooden shutters in front of the windows.

The single-pitch roof slopes towards the west and consists entirely of double-web Macrolon panels with wooden hinged slats. The roof slat position is selected to ensure that the low winter sun will heat the air above the collector chamber to provide room heating via a heat exchange process.

Photographs: Martin Classen

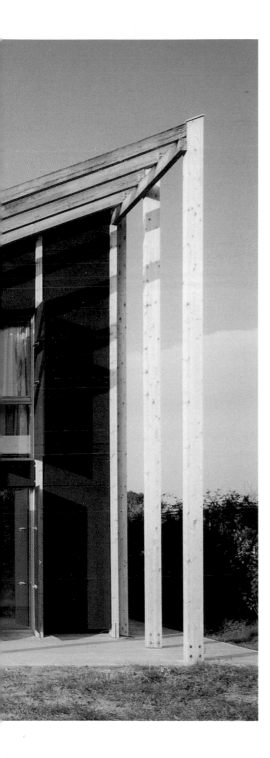

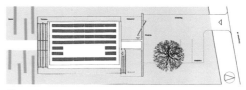

Site plan

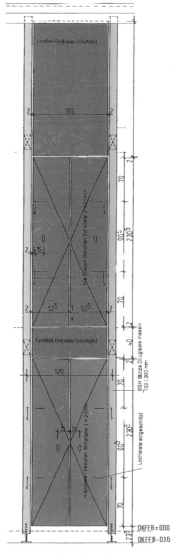

Detail of the east elevation shutters

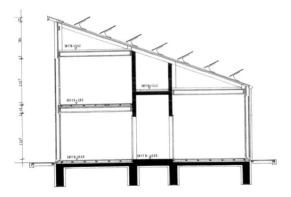

The roof, with a single slope towards the west, is comprised of double-weave Macrolon panels and strips of wood. The positions of the strips on the roof determines the amount of energy which will be used for the building's heating.

West elevation

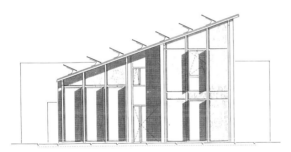

South elevation

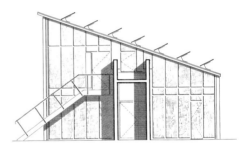

North elevation

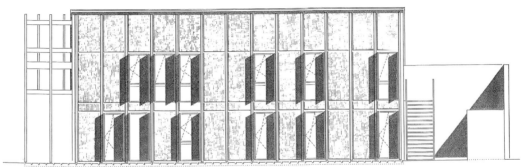

Section B-B

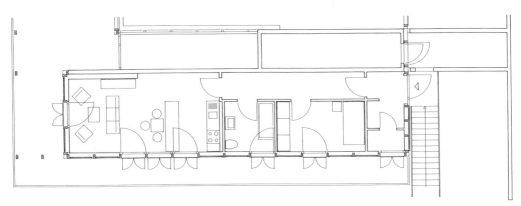

Upper floor plan

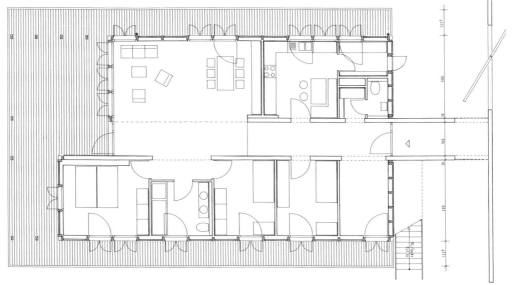

Ground floor plan

The tradition in greenhouse building was the departure point for this project, which is based on an autonomous ecological concept and aims to handle the dwelling's energy needs on a self-sufficient basis, free from outside help.

Construction detail

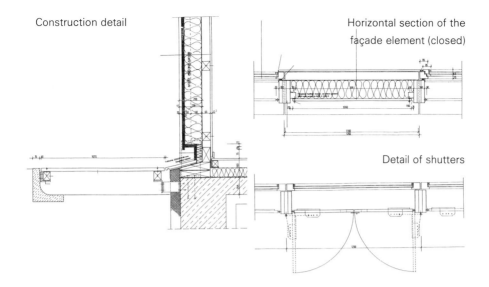

Horizontal section of the
façade element (closed)

Detail of shutters

Shigeru Ban
2/5 House
West Japan

The 49^{1}/$_4$ x 82 ft m rectangular plan of this house is divided into five zones each of 49^{1}/$_4$ x 16^{1}/$_2$ ft. From the south these zones are: front garden, interior space, central courtyard, a second interior space, back garden. The house is bounded on its east and west sides by two-story reinforced concrete walls.

In order to create the 2/5 (i.e. 2 by 1/5) first floor space, enclosed glass boxes, similar to that of Mies van der Rohe's Farnsworth House, were positioned across the second floor. The spaces created beneath these have a Japanese sensibility in which interior and exterior are linked both visually and physically. This contrasts with the merely visual spatial connectivity of Mies' work. The first floor is a "universal floor": a unified space within which each of the functional elements is placed, while at the same time the use of sliding doors at the boundary between interior and exterior, and the manually operated tent roof results in a sense both of enclosure and openness.

The screen on the road side is formed from bent, punched aluminum which folds up accordion-like to form the garage door. On the north side a grid of PVC gutters have been hung as planters, creating a dense screen which ensures privacy.

Photographs: Hiroyuki Hirai

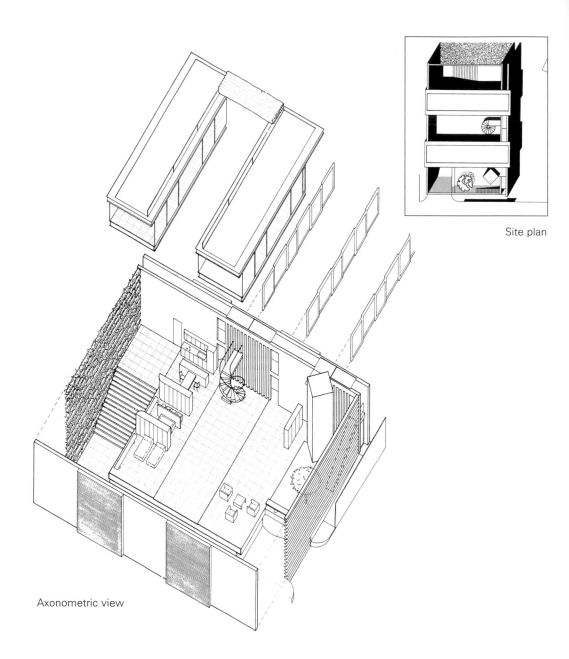

Site plan

Axonometric view

The façade of the dwelling that faces the street is clad with a sheet of perforated, corrugated metal that offers a high degree of privacy and creates a special visual connection with the exterior.

The combination of open and closed spaces on
the two floors results in dynamic atmospheres
that are visually connected and that adapt easily to the different uses that the residents may
require in the future.

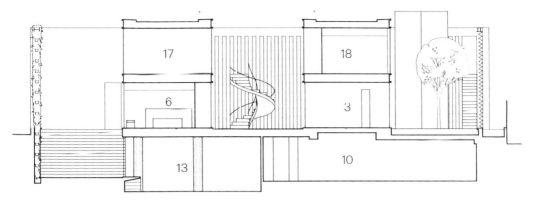

Section

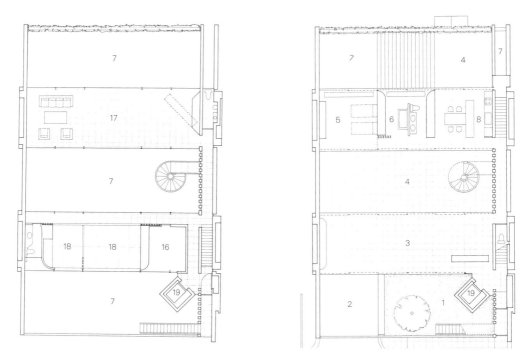

First floor plan

Ground floor plan

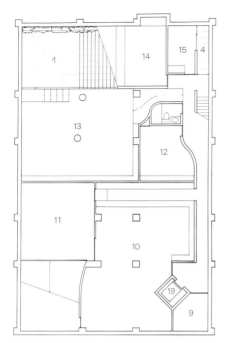

Basement floor plan

The spaces of the dwelling are impregnated with a Japanese sensibility, whose maximum expression is found in the delicate presence of the surrounding nature (the front and rear gardens) in the interior of the dwelling.

Thom Maine-Morphosis
Blades Residence
Santa Barbara, California, USA

In June 1990 several hundred homes in the coastal hills of Santa Barbara were destroyed by fire. The clients decided to reframe this catastrophic experience as a catalyst to reinvent their day-to-day existence. Unlike their neighbors who took more "conventional" approaches, they decided to build a house "like nothing they had ever seen before".

The fire left a charred landscape with a gentle sloping grade, several boulders and a cluster of native oaks. Given its suburban/rural context, the introspective strategy of an enclosed project was explored.

Due to the very modest budget, design and craftsmanship were given priority over expensive materials from the very first moment.

The 3,800 ft^2 interior spaces are organized as three main spaces adjacent to five smaller exterior rooms, each one a linear sequence of overlapping zones in which the boundaries of public and private spaces are intentionally blurred. Interior light is modulated through subtle openings and recesses that create a sculpted space.

The couple shares a very open bedroom, yet each has their individual studios at opposite ends of the house. The upper story studio enjoys wide views from a corner window that has been carved out, as well as an exterior catwalk. The ground floor studio/gallery is a separate wing with clerestory windows and no exterior views.

Photographs: Kim Zwarts

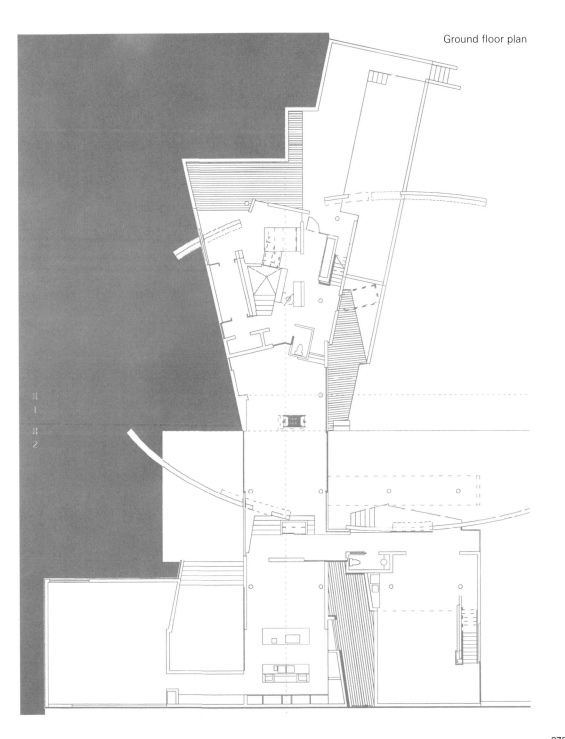

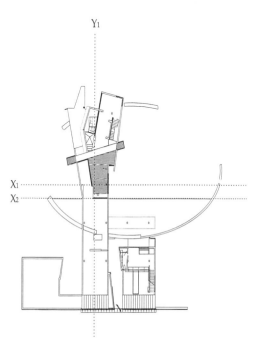

The internal and external volumes of the building overlap, forming a projection over the swimming pool.

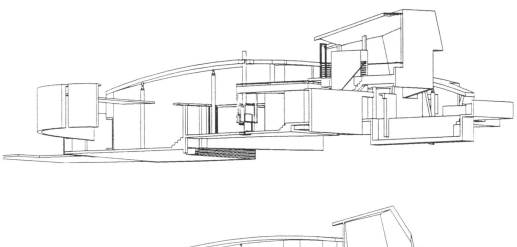

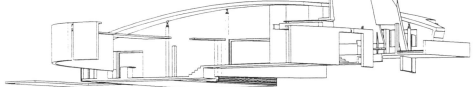

Cross sections

The interior of the dwelling is organized as a large bright single space that is completely uninterrupted.

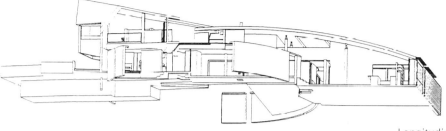

Longitudinal sections

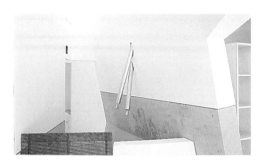

ARTEC Architekten
Raum Zita Kern
Raasdorf, Austria

Following the needs of the owner, a literature scholar who was fond of the country life, a new and provocative building element was constructed in the old farm of Marchfeld. The fundamental requirement was to create a large and comfortable office for reading and writing, far from the noisy atmosphere of the city. The conversion also required the construction of a bathroom and toilet and the installation of a complete heating system.

The starting point for the design was the former cow shed, the roof of which was in danger of caving in and had to be completely removed. The new roof was prolonged with the incorporation of a staircase located on the exterior, creating an unusual shape that marks the contrast between old and new. The original module was put to use as far as possible, so that the same building served as a basis for a new architectural element.

The whole façade of the cowshed is clad in aluminum, creating an experience that remains in the memory of its visitors. In the interior, materials such as poplar plywood and aluminum mark a certain distance from the rural atmosphere and provide a cosmopolitan and welcoming air.

The bathroom is located in the main building and is illuminated by a flat skylight. On it, the rainwater can collect up to a depth of two centimetres, thus creating special effects of shades.

The new office is located on the first floor, a space that is calm and distant from its surroundings and conducive to the full force of the intellect. This study opens onto two terraces through sliding doors that prolong the room even more. The location of the terraces helps illuminate the interior of the dwelling and makes a decisive contribution to the peculiar form of the scheme.

Photographs: Margherita Spiluttini

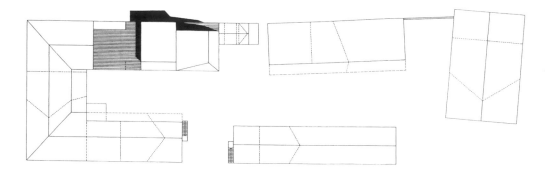

Site plan

The opposition between the construction materials of the old building and those used for the new space creates a special effect by merging the urban and rural atmospheres.

The impact achieved by incorporating aluminum into this old agricultural building helps integrate the rest of the buildings in this farm complex.

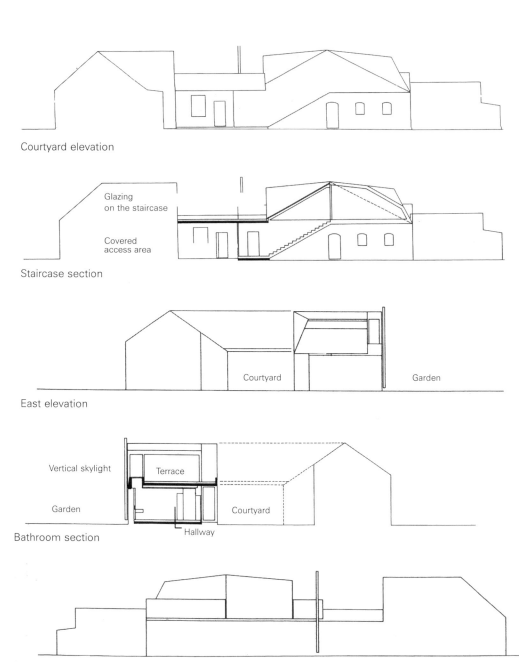

Courtyard elevation

Glazing
on the staircase

Covered
access area

Staircase section

Courtyard

Garden

East elevation

Vertical skylight

Terrace

Garden

Courtyard

Bathroom section

Hallway

North elevation

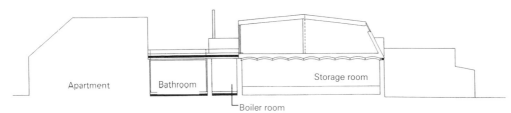

Apartment   Bathroom   Storage room

Boiler room

Section of the living room and terrace

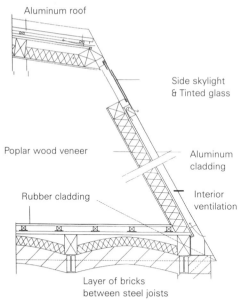

Aluminum roof

Side skylight
& Tinted glass

Poplar wood veneer

Aluminum
cladding

Rubber cladding

Interior
ventilation

Layer of bricks
between steel joists

Roof section

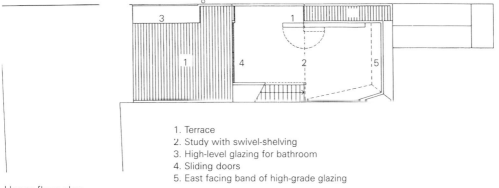

1. Terrace
2. Study with swivel-shelving
3. High-level glazing for bathroom
4. Sliding doors
5. East facing band of high-grade glazing

Upper floor plan

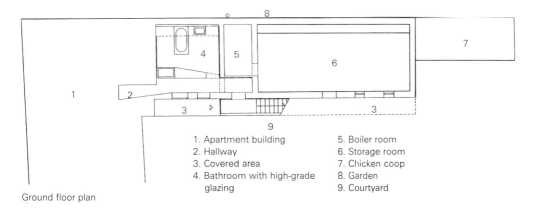

1. Apartment building
2. Hallway
3. Covered area
4. Bathroom with high-grade glazing
5. Boiler room
6. Storage room
7. Chicken coop
8. Garden
9. Courtyard

Ground floor plan